# A Matins Flywheel

*This book is for Jude Clarke  
and Jake Kennedy*

## Contents

### Matins for St. Agnes of the Crossroads: 62nd Avenue and 109th Street

| | |
|---|---|
| 12 | Matins 1, April 22, 2014 |
| 13 | Matins 2, Long Beach, October 25, 2014 |
| 14 | Matins 3, November 4, 2014 |
| 16 | Matins 4, December 1, 2014 |
| 17 | Matins 5, January 11, 2015 |
| 18 | Matins 6, January 14, 2015 |
| 19 | Matins 7, January 27, 2015 |
| 20 | Matins 8, April 9, 2015 |
| 21 | Matins 9: Persistence, January 5, 2016 |
| 23 | Matins 10, January 10, 2016 |
| 24 | Matins 11, January 11, 2016 |
| 26 | Matins 12, January 18, 2016 |
| 27 | Matins 13, January 24, 2016 |
| 28 | Matins 14, January 28, 2016 |
| 29 | Matins 15, February 4, 2016 |
| 30 | Matins 16, February 7, 2016 |
| 32 | Matins 17, February 18, 2016 |
| 34 | Matins 18, March 29, 2016 |
| 36 | Matins 19, March 30, 2016 |
| 38 | Matins 20, March 31, 2016 |
| 40 | Matins 21, April 4, 2016 |
| 41 | Matins 22, May 8, 2016 |
| 42 | Matins 23, June 8, 2016 |
| 43 | Matins 24, June 15, 2016 |

| | |
|---|---|
| 44 | Matins 25, June 22, 2016 |
| 45 | Matins 26, June 27, 2016 |
| 46 | Matins 27, June 28, 2016 |
| 47 | Matins 28, July 5, 2016 |
| 49 | Matins 29, July 7, 2016 |
| 50 | Matins 30, August 17, 2016 |
| 51 | Matins 31, September 27, 2016 |
| 52 | Matins 32, Wednesday, October 12, 2016 |
| 53 | Matins 33, October 25, 2016 |
| 54 | Matins 34, November 29, 2016 |
| 56 | Matins 35, March 26, 2017 |
| 57 | Matins 36, Friday, May 12, 2017 |
| 58 | Matins 37, May 25, 2017 |

## And Its Accompanying Flywheel

| | |
|---|---|
| 62 | Atomistic Plates: Your Father's Beat |
| 64 | Atomistic Plates: Your Father's Beat |
| 65 | Outside The Sylvia (1986) |
| 66 | Outside the Sylvia, Again (2016) |
| 70 | Have Yourself A Merry Little Christmas . . . (2002) |
| 75 | Atticus Riff (07/06/12) |
| 76 | All the Wrong People Are Going to Live Forever |
| 78 | Hat Trick: Impossible Subjects (Democracy/ Philosophy/ Love) |
| 87 | Prague Spring: A Quartet from 'Prague Spring: Twelve Cubist Sonnets,' 2008 |

. . . But now I'm suspecting that the working class person only knows how to make herself a more exalted kind of multiple. What's wrong with that. Growing up, adults always said: if I give it to you I will have to give it to everyone. Well give it to me I say. I am everyone. That's exactly who I am.
— Eileen Myles, *Inferno*

I was tired of so much thinking, which was what I did most in those days. I did other things, but I went on thinking while I did them. I might feel something, but I would think about what I was feeling at the same time. I even had to think about what I was thinking and wonder why I was thinking it.
— Lydia Davis, "The Professor"

I gently pump space into my chest which has been cramped for a long, long time, until the silence inside me matches the silence that surrounds me. I lie down again with my back in the pine needles, and it feels good to breathe the ice-cold air. I look up between the tree trunks to the sky, which is completely clear and full of stars, and it slowly turns around, the whole world turns slowly around and is a huge, empty space. Silence is everywhere, and there is nothing between me and the stars, and when I try to think of something, I think of nothing. I close my eyes and smile to myself.
— Per Petterson, *In the Wake*

Make the absolute visible and clear [ . . . ] the absolute is hidden but clear at the heart of the visible.
— Pierre Michon, "Bertran," *Winter Mythologies and Abbots*

# One

*Matins for St. Agnes of The Crossroads:*
*62nd Avenue and 109th Street*

*Matins 1, April 22, 2014*

As I was sitting on the couch this morning, staring out into a soft spring rain, listening to the CBC, I kept getting this sensation of vast canvases of portraits by Rubens and Rembrandt and Botticelli pivoting around me as I was sitting there . . . so you get this startling juxtaposition of the loopy unconfigured postmodern self plopped down smack dab in the middle of these romantic, renaissance and Elizabethan selves . . . no resolution . . . just a chronic juxtaposition that cannot be resolved . . . loads of cleverness in both fields, but no uber-claim as the dominant field . . . ah, Ozymandius, I tell ya . . . reading about the Russian formalist Shklovsky last night who realized, over the spectrum of his long life, the fragility of so-called cleverness, new theory, the experimental . . . the way the so-called 'new' becomes ho-hum each time, replaced as naturally as the waves coming in over the sand . . . Ozymandius' sand, of course . . . but those large, heaving portraits . . . how lush, how over-the-top, how abundant . . . how fatuous . . . but another kind of comfort . . . wheeling a Byzantine perpetual motion machine around me . . . clacking & whirring like flies . . . like gold . . .

*Matins 2, Long Beach, October 25, 2014*

Medieval or renaissance beach and ocean and wide sun-flooded sand stretches of beach flats — me walking out on them a new man: not just because I survived a quadruple bypass . . . but because of me, how I grew up, when I grew up: *that* kind of a new person in a new world. New eyes. De-romanticized but still flooded (as the sand) with a bright wonder you almost have to squint into to survive it is so beautiful. You almost wince from it. A kind of pain. And yet or *but* yet, I have this guide — this Welsh Springer Spaniel named Mosey — to lead me out onto these dazzling sand flats and into a new world and sun and rain and no enclosures caused by the mind (Blake's mind-forged manacles) enclosures of sentiment, patriotism, false honor, dysfunctional loyalties, empty gestures of love instead of love itself, instead of clarity itself, instead of sight itself. If we could only stay out here in the wind, or never forget standing here. While the surging tides pull us out and draw us in and we match that surge pulse for pulse, big-hearted, lungs full before the final dark, that all-encompassing dark love that is another kind of full. We are truly blessed, wonder-filled, wonder-full . . .

*Matins 3, November 4, 2014*

. . . praise and gratitude . . . funny how these old Catholic words might come back to 'literally' haunt me . . . praise and gratitude . . . I'm out walking Mosey this morning in the early morning humid mild fall Okanagan air . . . everything quiet . . . Mosey's head swaying below me from side-to-side, the rhythmic swinging encased by the plastic cowl he's been wearing since last Thursday when he had his significant operation . . . and my instinctive voice whispering, "That's a good dog . . . good old Mosey . . . " side to side as well, just above his radar, just above mine, too, because I'm not even aware of my voice until another human being crosses our path and I become, abruptly, self-conscious (but only momentarily), then lapse back into our side-to-side ritual once again . . . but the smell of the morning, its textures of concrete and damp grass and maple leaves collecting in every seam out here . . . soft and light and beautiful, whatever that means . . . but alive . . . pulsing . . . praise and gratitude . . . lately, in that other landscape — my head — a tumble of confusion and sadness and a kind of flatness I rarely experience . . . a flatness *like* sadness, but not the same . . . more cruel and less sweet than sadness . . . I know it's connected to something that shifted permanently in me when I got sick . . . I know it has to do with my getting a glimpse and a feel for the end of things . . . a kind of darkness I had never imagined before . . . a crazy, desperate leaving of everything behind . . . a silence that cannot be fathomed or, even, heard until you're embraced by it . . . and it's not all negative, though it sounds like it . . . not at all . . . but it can't be artificially redeemed or idealized or romanticized either . . . it is beyond what we try to resolve through words like positive and negative . . . it will have nothing to do with either of those words . . . instead, it's just waiting there like a great yawning charcoal vacuum . . . and you walk around in the face of it, and that walking around in the face of it affects everything else you're doing, all your dreams, your petty enthusiasms, your loves, your friendships, your relations and relationships . . . it lays on a skin of qualification, of hesitancy, of, not horror, but an almost appalling clarity that has to do with a parallel flatness in what we call the real or ordinary world . . . nothing like it . . . so you're stumbling along the street with this cowl around your body, your small dog leading you through this, your guide . . . and you're thinking, "OK. I can do this I guess," and another voice slips into the proceedings from the sidelines somewhere — in an unexpected rush of metaphysics and magic — and whispers, "Praise and gratitude, boy. Praise & gratitude." And you squint into the eastern morning sun and gulp down its logic and think, *yes*, it *is* praise and gratitude . . . that's what I'm here for: to love and acknowledge love, and praise and acknowledge the loves of the body, too, the elements, the micro-presences of whatever we used to mean by words like god, get down on my knees again near the end of my life, and in the face of this wheezing abundance, whisper *thank you* . . . here, on my knees in the early morning back alley, my eyes welling up in joy, not sorrow, the cowl lifting itself off to the light . . . my small dog a kite on a string, a pressure I can barely feel I am so unsubstantial . . .

*Matins 4, December 1, 2014*

Mosey & I at the BX Dog Park this morning. −12 degrees. No one out there but us at first. Three people showed up later. But I felt the presence of my best friend, George Larsen, this morning. He passed away too early in Edmonton last spring. Whenever I think of his presence, especially if I am out in a landscape, a spirit rushes through me, inexplicable. A metaphysical buzz, a transcendental shudder. He was my go-to guy that way. He was always further into it than I was, pulling me forward. So much of his view was housed in the subtlety and gracefulness and aesthetics of George's view of what is given and what is made. Both. What is given and what is made. And praise. We don't know anything. We think we do, but we don't. Praise. Celebrate. Love. The harder things. Make me an instrument . . . yes, that, too. And all of this leads me, by a strange circuitry, to Marilynne Robinson's thoughts on altruism and empathy in *Absence of Mind*. Vast. Endless.

I can't get past almost dying myself. It's really alive in me, just beneath the skin of everything I do. But I have to accept it or understand it better so I can be healthy through the time I *do* have left. I know I can get past it . . . I just never thought it would be so big. Is it depression? Or a clear sense of the limitations, the finiteness of all things? Stalling out in an acknowledgement of how we dream dreams to save us from this very sighting of absolute limitations, and then mistake those dreams for something else, for an artificial infinity. Immutability. I don't know. I wish I did. But I love everything right now and I guess I believe *that* love is infinite. I suspect that is the case.

*Matins 5, January 11, 2015*

Walking into the face of God . . . that's the recurring image/voice/whisper/blessing I kept getting this morning as Mosey and I trudged south through Marshal Fields, past the airport and along the creek to the lake. Small but continuous & firm tracks through the snow . . . Mosey bounding, me always balancing, balancing, gauging the surprises in the foundation path caused by the snow, a buoyant hesitancy defining the pilgrimage . . . pilgrimage . . . into the face of God . . . the image I kept getting was of a three-dimensional cut-out in the landscape and sky . . . if I held my balancing arms and legs out in a certain, clever, mysterious way, I would pass through a key-lock into paradise . . . walking right into and through the skin of God, the face of God . . . it's funny because I just started reading a book about Celtic wisdom last night — *Anam Cara* by John O'Donohue — and one of the first points he makes is that for the Celts there was no distinction between landscape and subjectivity . . . they were one and the same . . . so consciousness walks into consciousness and vice versa . . . how that all works with Don McKay's notion of wilderness and domesticity . . . so, when I say that I walked into the face of God, I may be saying that the most undomesticated part of me, the truly wildest part of me, walked into the most undomesticated part of God . . .

*Matins 6, January 14, 2015*

I read a sentence last night in Lydia Davis' novel, *The End of the Story*: "Maybe I did not want to have to choose a place to start, maybe I wanted all the parts of the story to be told at the same time." (11) Isn't that great? Thinking, of course, of the design of *The Kitchen Takes* . . . the seizure, structurally & syntactically, of a kind of simultaneity of unfolding . . . an illusion, but powerful . . . and maybe, in the end, not an illusion at all . . . up on the Grey Ditch Canal trail this morning in the snow . . . with Jude & Mosey . . . stumbling into a white you cannot differentiate anything in . . . so there are few borders if you look down . . . you cannot judge the space . . . you must simply exist & persist as forward motion . . . the acceleration of the heart . . . man ascending, man descending, soul ascending, soul descending . . . lost in the jazz of it . . . listening to Glen Gould's *Goldberg Variations* right now . . . yes . . . metafiction incarnate . . . his irresistible, gorgeous mumbling voice-over works for me . . . like snow . . . and I guess, in the end, you have to admit that you didn't have a lot of company . . . that was the big price paid . . . oh, you *thought* you were going to have a lot of company, but it turned out you didn't . . . ah well . . . it's just that your world of referencing becomes so small eventually and, possibly inaccessible precisely when you don't want it to be . . . you want it to be big and accessible . . . that hurt & loss contained in Michael Keaton's eyes when he conjured up his family in his Golden Globe acceptance speech for *Birdman* . . . always just too late . . . the acoustics of snow . . .

*Matins 7, January 27, 2015*

Bill Evans. "My Foolish Heart" . . . wild . . . bewildered . . . love it . . . just in from a long walk with Mosey on Marshal Fields . . . he's acting out now, trapped in the front foyer, desperate, driving *me* crazy . . . talk about choosing our 'wildernesses,' . . . very funny . . . though Jude is floundering re: the pain in her feet these days, the two of us are still rattling around these pre-kidney-transplant days enjoying *everything* (as Lou Reed might say) . . . it's true . . . each day, itself . . . this morning, as I entered the Bean Scene, Ross Fety was sitting at an outside table, smiling, and he said each morning was simply an unfolding of grace and it was our luck to be in it . . . yes, yes, yes . . . then, out in Marshal Fields, I thought again so much of my mom and dad and where they are in the universe aside from the consciousnesses of their seven children . . . life and death, its mysteries, eh? . . . each morning an unfolding of grace . . . it's density we want . . . we don't *just* want to be entertained . . . we want the complexity and nuance of density . . . that's what we also want . . . we don't *expect* it, mind you . . . but it's what we want . . . the ad guys have it wrong . . . Mulroney's vision of an endless free market whose energy vortex is the lowest common denominators of quality & quantity . . . that is *not* what we want . . . we might have to *be* in that market . . . we might have to *survive* in it even . . . but it's not what we want at all . . . density, the other elusive grail . . . *san graal* . . . *sang raal* . . .

*Matins 8, April 9, 2015*

*Because my brother Michael sent me a clip of Nancy Wilson, singing . . .*

In a YouTube clip of an ancient 1964 TV appearance, Nancy Wilson performs her version of "The Very Thought of You," and I'm listening so hard to her phrasing, her breath, until, finally, the music, as sumptuous as the melody of this song *is*, surrenders its lovely and considerable machinery over to the mere voice telling an impossibly intimate story. I think of poetry, naturally, and the function of surprise. I remember reading somewhere once that Michael Ondaatje had confessed he 'wanted to be changed' when he read a poem. That's what he expected. I used to regale my writing students with this anecdote because I thought it was so beautiful and so frightening at the same time. Over the years, I suspect I refined his comment so that each time I sit down to write, I try to write until I surprise myself. Just look at Nancy Wilson leaning forward now into the mic, gesturing with both arms after singing the intro, suspended over the real start of the song now . . . just watch her body, her shoulders, as she lilts for the first time into the words, "The very thought of you." Incredible suspension. And in spite of any predictably contrived effects around it and in it, her body collapses at this very point into a sure, almost trance-like improvisation of the words, and her gorgeous, misshapen, always fluctuating mouth goes on to twistingly tell the wonderful story of her love. I cannot believe the way she handles, as a singer, word clusters like, "the mere idea of you." The weight on idea. The way she draws out the idea of idea until the very charcoal limits of my own spring morning here fifty-three years later are swept away in a spring rinse of thought, of carbon and time and generation and regeneration and ideas of ideas, and as the world collapses outside my window into its very limit, Nancy Wilson's voice is a thin, reedy balsam from somewhere behind or beneath everything else I am letting go of, all that bulky fumbling thinking as, instead, I watch my hand stretching itself away from and toward the release of everything it used to touch and try to claim. Of you. Whatever in the dust of it you are. The very.

*Matins 9: Persistence, January 5, 2016*

> "... *by figuring the world as it is lived rather than as it is seen.*"
> — Melissa Ragain, in her introduction to *Dissolve into Comprehension: Writings and Interviews, 1964—2004,* Jack Burnham, Cambridge: The MIT Press, 2015

My next door neighbor is scraping last night's snow off his cedar-shingled roof with a long improvised attachment he's jimmied onto a conventional plastic shovel. At first, out of the corner of my eye — all peripheral, where the magic is, where the truth is — I thought some crows or magpies were up to something on the roof . . . but then I saw the rhythm of the movements, and the calculated, contrived persistence of those movements, and something in me, without thinking about it, recognized movements that were designed, movements that were human . . . he's done now . . . the roof is clear . . . and I am still sitting here deep in words, stuck in them, almost buried, staring out into the three inches of fresh snow expanding and enlarging every object in my yard, all the low shrubs and sucker maples and poplars that I've allowed to grow wild (except that I cut them back twice a year) along the disintegrating fence that separates us . . . there! . . . my goofy eighteen-month-old Welsh Springer Spaniel has just and suddenly bounced in from the right side of this tableau and is a red and white disturbance like the snow, and like the snow, too, in that he is both direct and, sometimes, just something necessary and precious I sense on the sidelines of my sight, breathing somewhere in a periphery of slightly unregistered but always kinetic, things . . .

I found these two photos from my childhood yesterday . . . my mother had tucked them away for me before she passed away . . . same notion as the peripheral when you stop to examine them . . . or her . . . same magic unfolding somewhere else, but always somewhere close . . . language, eh? . . . but there we are, in both photos, playing hockey . . . In the first photo, my brother and I and three friends are playing hockey in our backyard, on a rink my father had stayed up all night to make for us . . . I remember the making of the rink because of the logic of the physics in the act itself, something my father explained (possibly, instinctively, a guy thing, whatever that means now) . . . but he explained that because of the fierce cold in Edmonton in the winter, you couldn't ever leave the hose alone if you were flooding the cleared yard to make a rink . . . the hose could quickly and drastically freeze, close up, and the worst case scenario might be a backup of ice that could end up breaking your pipes and flooding your house in January . . . so my dad stayed up all night, patiently flooding the rectangle in the snow he had cleared . . . he knew what he was doing . . . we were sure of him in this . , , we were hypnotized . . . even a bit nauseous . . . the gold of it, the magical incarnation of it . . . to make something out of nothing . . . that mirror of the sky . . . *hoc est enim corpus meum* . . . the mass of my childhood flooding back to me this morning as I stare out into this snow now and for no reason . . . well, not exactly true . . . come on . . . I sense Dylan Thomas' voice falling all around me, like another snow:

> *And to fall asleep into that cantilevered dream of Edmonton back then when Harry and I were turning, cutting circles into the crisp night air beneath Orion and Cassiopeia, beneath the Northern Lights, our tube skates knifing the ice surface out in the backyard on the twenty by thirty foot rink Dad has made for us, him standing out there through the January night before, smoking cigarettes to entertain himself, thinking his self into a myriad of parallel lives flickering all around him through the night air in that maze of everything else that is possible (maybe, even especially, me showing up in that thick, uncontrived-ness and looking back and thanking him . . . me, from now, that is) . . . smoking those cigarettes in the dark, only their red glow visible from time to time through the basement window where we were watching him, his sons, our eyes full . . .*

And in both photos, unseen, unregistered, those power poles in a distance, hovering over us, their fine wire weaving a sparkling dark hum above our heads that we might never see or hear because it is so present, so close by . . .

*Matins 10, January 10, 2016*

Sometimes, in the sifting sideways thick of the most trivial of intersections, the most banal and over-stuffed moments when nothing seems to be happening and instead you sense you are waiting, waiting for something like life and movement to be born or arrive, sometimes in the dull intransigent flatness of such moments, I sense in the underside of their nothingness, *everything* . . . I sense that I can almost hear the beat of that everything, its design, and this sensation is so exhilarating, so palpable sometimes, that I start to snap my fingers to it, then clap my hands together at some delayed after-rhythm, some backbeat of love and universe and you, whoever you are . . . and I wake up and I'm Rory Block suddenly, playing her version of 'Walking Blues' and 'Death Letter' to the ten-thousand people standing on the burial ground of that old flatness, the song and the people lowering such flatness into a dark carbon rinse of time . . .

Matins 11, January 11, 2016

Sitting here this morning, overwhelmed by the idea of mediocrity. Not in a vicious, petty, or angry way, but in a strangely human & empathetic way. Maybe it's my age. Maybe it's my own unique circumstances: I have been involved, since my early twenties, in the pursuit of success and/or failure in at least two art forms that have the unresolveable puzzle of both commercial and artistic success at the hearts of their composition: writing and music. And because of Jude's health, and my own health since 2013, I have also been artificially removed and distanced from those worlds — like a ZOOM camera can withdraw from a scene — and as a consequence I have a unique, distanced perspective or lens to peer through that reveals those worlds in a clarity I don't really want to experience sometimes.

I don't know.

But, as Ebenezer confesses through Alistair Sims, at least I *know* that I don't know . . . anyway, I'm going to take this on slowly over the next year, this 'ascent of the midlings', because I am worried that a natural conflict of interest, driven by the urgency of commercial success, has finally not only *appropriated* notions of artistic success and integrity — witness the migration of words like innovation, creativity, passion, improvisation, authenticity, humility into the bosom(s) of the business and commercial worlds — but has appropriated them so successfully that such a conflict of interest has now become *invisible*, even forgotten. But it's the *addiction* it represents that must be stopped because, like all addictions, it prevents something else that is real and innocent and intensely human and complex and good from happening; it prevents a real artistry from surfacing or even being conceived and instead, we nod out in the heavy crack trance of artificial satisfaction, endless mediocrity convincing us of its authenticity just like booze does, just like cocaine does, just like junk or food or sex can, too. Substitution. Copy. Simulacrum. We have to stop this train so we can restore vigor to ourselves, to our art forms, the way we keep vigilant about sports. We'd never let professional sports to get lazy or mediocre like this. It wouldn't happen. They'd never get away with it there. And the strange thing there is that the biggest insurance policy *against* mediocrity *is* commercial interest itself. It *insists* on certain levels of quality . . . something absent in the artistic world.

I don't know.

But I do.

*Matins 12, January 18, 2016*

Just this niggling thought that I used to be a particularly 'nice' person, but I'm not anymore. And I know it's not true, and I know it's connected somehow to that heavy dose of general anaesthetic plus oxycontin I had to take three years ago to survive that surgery — and which induced a kind of low-grade paranoia. It'll be all right. I think I'm past it. It's my refusal to play a false role now re: affection and admiration that has made the difference. And I like that difference. It's not going away. And that's OK. It's OK.

*Matins 13, January 24, 2016*

*Sometimes I get lost in my body for days and days and days.*

Yes, still and precisely . . . and a soft but heavy blanket of melancholy and/or low-grade depression advances and encloses the sight, the ability to see . . . perspective . . . was reading this stunning little book today — stunning because of its thoughtfulness about its subject and the subtlety of its awareness of its own form — Colm Toibin's book, *On Elizabeth Bishop* . . . and it's the comments he makes about restraint in poetry, about the play with absence and presence and some of Bishop's strategies from that point of view, that knock me out, make me think . . . and it is such a relief to read something that is so deliberately free of any motive other than celebration and, especially, the celebration of complexity in art. Reading Toibin is like listening to a classical musician speak of Bach . . . you hear this excitement and urgency in a world being taken over by only copies of that, a manufactured, calculated rhetoric of authenticity that couldn't be more distanced from its actual subject. Yes, it gives you hope. And for me, on this low-fog January morning in the midst of my own predictable winters, reading Colm Toibin is a sanctuary I can retreat into for a bit . . .

*Matins 14, January 28, 2016*

Oh my God yes, he said, yes to everything. Yes to everything. This soft dove-grey morning, the fragrance of spring just one layer away from everything, the early light full of that promise. Colm Toibin's beautiful book on Elizabeth Bishop and her poetry, I have to say I love the landscape of this book. It is very much like the late winter landscape around me right now here in this mountain valley, a David Milne ecstasy. Small, precise meditations and/or probes prompted by an image, a tone, a phrase. I don't always agree with him — especially his attachment to things as metaphors instead of things themselves — but that's wonderful, too, and it opens up these quiet winter morning dialogues in other ways. You betcha! I am tired and I don't know why. I suspect I need to push myself more physically. And some peevish, anarchic side of me thinks, "What the fuck!" And is resisting. But I'll get out there walking again. I will. Mercy, as Leonard Cohen might say.

*Matins 15, February 4, 2016*

Heavy snow through the night . . . a dazzling winter wonderland again this morning . . . everything big with white and ideas of perfection and redemption . . . a heavy snowfall will do it every time . . . am near the end of that great little book of essays by Colm Toibin . . . I love reading something this thoughtfully, this artfully done . . . he is so aware of how the logic of his own meditations, the forms of them, suggest, echo or imitate his subject. It really knocks me out, even if I disagree with him, because I also agree with him all over the place and love to watch his mind process things. Here he is talking about what Elizabeth Bishop valued in Hopkins: *Hopkins, she wrote, "has chosen to stop his poems, set them to paper, at the point in their development where they are still incomplete, still close to the first kernel of truth or apprehension which gave rise to them."* He is trying to explain, eventually, qualities of both kinesis and tentativeness in Bishop's poems, qualities that increase a sense of immediacy or urgency based in the movement that is *in* the moment of awareness rather than Wordsworth's looking back at it, processing it later.

*Matins 16, February 7, 2016*

When I was a boy and a young man growing up on the southside of Edmonton in the 50s and 60s, I was raised, along with my six brothers and sisters, in a close-knit Roman Catholic parish called St. Agnes. There were probably two or three hundred families in that parish and we were one of the smaller families. It was after the war, and there was a great sense then that young couples had to re-populate a new and better world for the future. Somehow, and I know this didn't happen everywhere else, that better world was envisioned as an international world in Edmonton, not a parochial one. It might have been a vision sewn somewhere in those fields our young fathers had fought in, or maybe it was conceived in a more capricious and hard-to-see mix of immigration and opportunity that had unraveled in cities like Edmonton since the first world war had ended. I'm not sure, but by the early 50s in Edmonton there was a rich mix of British, Scottish, Irish, Ukrainian, Russian, Polish, German, Hungarian, Czechoslovakian, Jewish, Chinese, Japanese, and Aboriginal Canadians. Except for a couple of famous football players hired by the Edmonton Eskimos — players like Rollie Miles and Johnny Bright — there were almost no African Americans in Edmonton then, and it wasn't until the 70s that East Indian and Pakistani families began to arrive. But in some fundamental ways, Edmonton *did* feel like the beginnings of a new world back then. It really did. I'd wander its cosmopolitan winter streets in a trance, thinking of my own future, and imagining all of us doing great things and finding happiness in different ways. I have to admit there was a fundamental and complex modesty at the base of all this imagining, but it still got dreamed up anyway. I sometimes weep at the memory of that boy walking those streets and dreaming those dreams. Sometimes on Saturday afternoons or evenings I'd help out at the St. Agnes Church Bazaar or its Whist nights. I'd talk to the Olsens, the Trepaniers, the Mohers, the Schmidts, Mrs. Kroetsch and Mrs. Pasternak — all the parents who had quietly watched over us, conspiring to do things for us whether it was coaching us at hockey or driving us to summer camps. I liked talking to them. And I don't know what it was about them, but these parents forestalled a self-consciousness and vanity in me that I could have assumed as a teenager, but which I didn't assume. I couldn't put on any airs or be condescending or stuck up with these people. And this became a reflex that never changed in my life, no matter where I lived or what I did or achieved — in Edmonton, Toronto, Regina, Nelson or Vernon — I simply could never indulge in that kind of vanity. It wasn't part of my makeup because of those parents back there in St. Agnes. I indulged in all sorts of *other* bad things, and could be an asshole in many ways, easily, but never in *that* way . . . do you know what I mean? And when I got lucky and went to U of A for six years, then York University in Toronto for another three, when I realized I was going to teach College and University students, and become an artist myself, a writer, I could still never break that fundamental reflex. The further I was drawn into *avant garde* aesthetics and experimental poetry and fiction even, the more fiercely I clung to this perspective I had acquired as a child and young adult. I could never make art for the vain ones, the hipsters, the second guessers, the restless pretend artists, the excluders, the ones who were perpetually stylish but afraid to risk Lou Reed's 'everything.' I never felt comfortable in any art worlds that encouraged safe hiding places for the ego, safe distances. I came, eventually, to be even wary of irony, though I was often buried alive in it myself. And I kept making art for an audience I knew wouldn't put up with me for a second in my own adult life. And it was true. The older I got and the more books I published — even if those books were *about* them, which they always were — the more wary they became of me, wary and suspicious even. I expected that. I knew the score. I was on the other side. It was easy to see.

But I didn't care really. I made art for them anyway. They had placed me where I was. They had given me everything to get me there. All I could do to honour them was raise up slab and hallucinatory mirrors to catch the light of their love and dignity and throw these things back out onto the very fields they had prepared for me. I don't make art for the vain ones, the hipsters, even though I love them, too. I just can't. And that inability keeps me right here, glancing sideways into the sun hanging and fracturing and flooding millions of dust motes through the bevelled basement west windows of a St. Agnes' Church Bazaar on a desultory March Saturday afternoon in 1963. We're halfway to Easter here today. I am imagining spring through my fifteen-year-old body. I can smell the fragrance of it that comes right from the newly exposed dirt itself and the scent of rain rinsing the snow earlier this morning. Everything's about to happen *again*. I'm exactly where I'm supposed to be.

*Matins 17, February 18, 2016*

Have been lost in two Per Petterson novels: *In the Wake* and *It's Fine By Me*. I read *Out Stealing Horses* and I've ordered *To Siberia*. He fascinates me. I tried to explain why to Jake earlier this morning: it's because Petterson presents a very textured compression, but he places this compression — somehow — within a larger, culturally referenced context so that we get a tricky, even impossibly intricate microcosm whirling within an accessible macrocosm, a macrocosm that is indistinct, but just visible enough to provide the intense pleasure of the universal. Berger does it. Michon does it. Jake does it in *Hazard*. I've reached for it many times, but especially in *Wood Lake Music* and *The Face in the Garden*. Ondaatje does it, especially in *The Collected Works of Billy the Kid*. Richard Ford in *Wildlife*. Kristjana Gunnars in *The Prowler*. But it's tricky, tricky, tricky. It doesn't run on 'correspondences.' Correspondences are Baudelaire, Joyce & Lowry machines. No, they're not a net of correspondences. Instead, they're a net of faintness, subtlety — titles, allusions, echoes, quotes, shameless gags — all nudges toward the macrocosm, towards the lineages we are writing out of. We are writing out of those lineages the same way jazz musicians are playing out of their lineages . . . with intense technical & spiritual awareness, love, and an almost sacred sense of joy and honoring. Hard to explain. And it can't be too mechanical. That would kill it and make it self-conscious. It has to be gracefully done, confidently done, almost like a kind of improvisation. An early example for me might be my honoring of Wallace Stevens in a poem in *Frieze* called "Incarnation Quartet: Sunday Mornings". So the title sets the macrocosm up, and so does this line: "Not this wide and indifferent blue," directly from Stevens' argument. Without the title, and without that slight, but key echo at the start, the reader's experience would be different. Wallace Stevens' poem "Sunday Morning" becomes a quiet, faint cradle that surrounds my own poem and, even, supports its logic. My poem a microcosm whirling within a faintly suggested macrocosm. In Ford's *Wildlife*, it's just the fuse of the 'wildlife' metaphors that constitute the macrocosm. This is what Petterson has borrowed from Richard Ford in *It's Fine By Me*. These two sixteen-year-old boys, caught in a microscopic *bildungsroman* that vibrates eventually as a universal. Blah, blah, blah. But here is something crucial that is often ignored in criticism of literature: there is a tendency to suspect a snooty kind of academic self consciousness in art that purposefully *refers* to other art. I've certainly been misread that way, especially responses to *Wood Lake Music*. But the references in my poem — the web of echoes that make up the macrocosm I'm referring to here (above) — those references aren't there to *save* or *rescue* the piece by *borrowing* culture that is more *significant* than the piece itself; no; they're there in order to spotlight the piece itself, allow the reader to see its unique, microcosmic significance. Hard to explain. But very true, I suspect. They're there as the klieg lights you've set up for an installation. Or a web of lazer beams you need to arrange carefully in order to create a hologram. They're there, quite naturally, as allusions in jazz improvisations. And no one would ever question that in jazz. They're not snooty at all.

*Matins 18, March 29, 2016*

*Clear browsing data.* Right. The old, stuffed hard drive. My internal hard drive. I am sitting in the soft green chair, staring out into the town in the thick of this late March morning here in the mountains, trying to get back to that freshness there always seemed to be in those moments, trying to clear the storage so there is nothing but focus and clarity. Nothing but love. Interesting when you do that. Sure, it *is* a reach for redemption. That *is* what is going on. No doubt about it. But why not reach for redemption? Just the simple hope for those fresh eyes says something about what the human condition is anyway: that we not only need those eyes to renew love, but that we are capable of making it happen, of being able to go back almost, and recreate that first seeing . . . and even the re-creation, even that itself, becomes another aspect of what exists. Itself is something we might reach back for farther on down the line.

Just finished *To Siberia*, the fifth Per Petterson novel in a row. He is a magnificent writer. I will pop the last paragraph of this novel into these notes here because it is so stunning. I wondered where he'd go. And there he went. Simply stunning, just as a paragraph, a set of words, a microcosm. There is a lot of Richard Ford's *Wildlife* in *To Siberia* and *It's Fine By Me* and *In the Wake*. All I mean by that is that in each case, a supposedly straightforward plot is so encased in a set of stunning, simple images that curls around the plot and holds it, that the whole thing is beating, in your palm. In this one, the image of Siberia. Stunning stuff. Lifts the heart.

More, later.

[Here's that last paragraph in Petterson's *To Siberia*:

*I went up the quay past the steps to the hotel. I saw a man through the window with a beer in his hand, and another man with a basket full of eggs. I was feeling heavy now, and tired, and I stood there leaning backward with my hands crossed behind my back at the end of the breakwater before I walked on to the beach on the other side and some way along on the hard-frozen white sand. It had started to blow a bit, and it was still cold with no snow, so I took off my scarf and tied it around my head and ears and sat down in the shelter of a dune and blew into my hands to warm them before I lit a cigarette. Poker ran along the edge of the water with a seagull's wing in his mouth, and I was so young then, and I remember thinking: I'm twenty-three years old, there is nothing left in life. Only the rest.]*

*Matins 19, March 30, 2016*

I didn't realise, or couldn't know how hurt I had been, how wounded. 'Didn't' because I just stumbled forward, as we all do, accepting conditions and hoping for better ones. Or 'couldn't' because the forces inflicting the hurt were too hard to see, too vast, too complex. So the fact that this knowledge is being given to me now, in my sixties, is a strange, mixed gift. I welcome it as knowledge, but I am fully aware that such knowledge brings with it an attendant price of seriousness and weariness even, and those things can overtake your story, bleach your instinctively gutsy sense of humor about these things. Ah well, it's only your whole life we're talking about here. No big deal. See what I mean? Tricky.

The other side of this knowledge is the knowledge of how lucky I have been. Me and my family. We've had luck and richness raining down on us the whole time. Crazy bastards. Shuffling around in the doorway, bluffing to get in. Always grinning. Always up to something. When I rounded the corner to visit my mother in the hospital just before she died, she cocked her head warily at me as she took me in. "What are *you* doing here?" she asked, fully aware that if I had flown all the way from the Okanagan to see her, she was in more trouble than she'd thought. I was like the grim reaper showing up at the foot of her bed, smiling some creepy, harvesting grin. But we'd both laughed and laughed. That's what it was always like with her. Lovely.

The sun was new this morning, screeching in quietly as a truly spring sun. Licking its way into all the corners and seams of 25th Street, the street where I walk for four kilometers every morning. And I was trying, in my own way, to be as new as it was, as fresh and as powerful. Texture on texture. The awareness of light and heat: the real beauty of the body in time, the aesthetics of it, the poise, the grace . . . the only things that matter in the end.

Even the hurt doesn't matter. It just blends in. Serves the rest. It is just another surface, another texture, unfolding itself inside out to the morning and the sun and the light. The hurt doesn't matter in this sun. It matters in other ways. It matters if it interferes with this morning. That's when it matters. It matters if it is stealing something away from you again, as it did the first time, some birthright, some dignity, some love. That's when it matters. That's when it becomes political.

Now we're talking.

*Matins 20, March 31, 2016*

Joining. Joinery. "Joinery is a part of woodworking that involves joining together pieces of timber or lumber, to produce more complex items." Seams. Stitches. Joins. We were talking about art the other morning, Jude and I, and I blurted out that everything had to do with seams and joins. Predictably ridiculous comment, right out of the blue. Typical. *Non sequitur.* But I had been thinking for days about the *construction* of things, the *composition* of things, from concrete structures to abstract structures, and I think I had begun to understand something I had been working on instinctively, for years, in my own writing: the intricate, subtle and almost frighteningly important art of joinery. Knowing where the breaks are, the seams are. Knowing how to allow panels to exist side by side and still stand, joined, independent but linked. These things *are* important. The glue of structure. Where the breaks are, the seams are. And just as crucial, where they are in the world *before* they exist as the rhythm for an artistic object. So you think, for example, of the simple notion of story, of narrative. And you stare into the original circuitry *in the world*, and then you imagine an alternate, complimentary, or more magical *corresponding* circuitry *in the art*. Another, beautiful world. And you imagine where the seams are, the breaks, the joins. Same thing in poetry. Where these things are in the world, and then, where they might be in that other, crazy, but gorgeous world of, literally, earthly delights. *Incarnation.* The word made flesh. *Hoc est enim corpus meum.*

Three arborists are over in the house behind us this morning, dismantling a one-hundred-year-old maple that has become too old, too weak in its limbs after years of inexpert pruning. You know how it is. It happens all the time, even here in a valley of orchards. They are disassembling the tree from top to bottom, a reversal of its slow growth, whatever that means. They will take it down to the nub of its roots, even pulverizing the roots. A complete deconstruction. A collapse. An unfolding. Erasure. One hundred years collapsing around me in a meticulously orchestrated circuitry of structure and joins. "Counselling decision, decision . . . " William Stafford's sharp swallows swerving, "flaring and hesitating, hunting for the final curve" in his wondrous poem, "The Well Rising". Decisions. Where the seams are. The joins, the breaks. Decisions.

On the wall to the left of my desk, I have a beautiful black and white photo of my grandfather, John Hugh Brown, the man I was named after. In the photo my grandfather is in his eighties and he is in his office, fixing a clock. After his own jewelry store collapsed in 1929 because of the fall of the stock markets in North America, my grandfather worked for the CPR, fixing clocks. He also refereed professional hockey in the Maritime league, and was so good at it that when he was retiring they got him to referee a game between Boston and Montreal. That kind of eye, eh? Something precise in his gaze that allowed him to calibrate things. Of course, all these possible metaphors are now beginning to pull away from one another's logic. *Non sequitur*. But regardless of such dissolution occurring in my own attempt to force a join, it is true to say that one hundred years ago today, my grandfather, my mother's father, was a young married man living with his wife and two daughters in Moncton, New Brunswick. My mother, Adrienne, would be born into this family six years later, in 1922. She would give birth to me in 1948. The limbs. The seams. The joins. This architecture. Collapsing. Decision, decision.

*Hoc est enim corpus meum.*

"I place my feet/with care in such a world."

*Matins 21, April 4, 2016*

Just a sketch here this morning, of some flash I don't want to forget. I want to come back to it. But we watched *The Big Short* on Friday night. I really enjoyed it. I could quibble re: the structure of it, and some issues with clarity & juxtaposition, but I really admired it, especially what it was trying to *see* . . . wonderful, wonderful . . . then, waking up the next morning I realized there was something *else* about it — incarnate in Steve Carrel's character's rage — that made it a perfect, microcosmic metaphor for what has happened in the art world over the exact same period . . . from the early 70s 'till now . . . the same bogus investments, overrated, bloated dogshit wrapped in catshit stuff — *the ascent of the midlings* . . . so as a way of explaining the fatuous bankruptcy of the so-called commercial centre in fiction for example, you simply draw an analogy to the fraudulent ratings given to sub-prime mortgages . . . and the equivalent creation of a bubble that has to burst eventually and reveal itself — though everything will be done to avoid those revelations . . . so, if you let art be run by arts administrators and agents and marketers, eventually the same grand-scale bankruptcy ensues and implodes, collapsing in on itself . . .

*Matins 22, May 8, 2016*

A sunny but blustery Monday morning . . . slow start . . . things very good lately re: Jude's feet . . . but we're still stuck in this strange, limbo-like, undefined transitional state of being as two people with hope and two people, artists, trying to live in a small city like Vernon and not be completely swamped by all the cruel, false comparisons presented by the lives of the peers around us . . . in my worst moments I fear that I will live out my last days trying to lead a life I'm not good at, always coming up a bit short as the retired, jockish, middle-class guy who wants to clean his barbecue every couple of days . . . shit . . . I've never been able to be that guy . . . why not be the person you're *good* at being instead? . . . a singer, a writer, a guy who laughs a lot because he *doesn't* take anything too seriously . . . blah, blah, blah . . . but there isn't much company for that guy here . . . not really . . . and that's not a snobby or elite thing to say . . . it's just real . . .

*Matins 23, June 8, 2016*

Dad's birthday tomorrow. June 9. Twenty-five years gone. Wizard man. Beautiful man. He raised me in a modesty so rich and complicated I have always been paralyzed by the possible transgressions of greed harboured accidentally in the self. Fear of the power of the self.

I've been walking around lately in a paroxysm of reinvention and exploration. Each morning unfolds like some sacred linen napkin set aside for me. Four-cornered. Sure. That's fine. Every thing is like a burning bush, so much so that I wonder sometimes, deep in the moment, if I'm about to die. I can't seem to account for the acute clarity otherwise . . . but then I do not die . . . and the next burning bush appears, an ashtray thrown in the ditch off the asphalt road, a weed my dog has shit on, the slick surface of the plastic bag over my hand that is now picking up that shit, the heat in the fresh shit itself, the sky, my eye looking back at me abruptly from the rear-view mirror, some old tape with Marshall McLuhan's voice whispering to me something crazily obscure about the rear-view mirror itself and all its possible metaphors, talismans for everything that is happening suddenly around me, this blessing like water, like baptism, this catechism of belief that wasn't belief until a few moments ago just as my dog Mosey grinned at me in the same mirror from the back of the car where I keep him prisoner sometimes though he forgives me. Sure. That's fine, too.

*Matins 24, June 15, 2016*

They're most of them gone now, and the world has changed.

I'm railing on about the need for modesty and empathy and altruism, but maybe the truth is my imagination or consciousness might be caught back in another audience. It's possible. Maybe I'm getting it all wrong or seeing it all wrong. I don't know. And maybe there's a law, like a law of physics, that kicks in naturally when you reach a certain age and induces a kind of mute button on your voice and an invisibility button on your presence, and insures you cannot communicate with people who are younger, who are three or four layers or waves after you, or behind you. Do you know what I mean? It also induces an urgency in you that is innocently misinterpreted as some almost predictable and cute curmudgeonly coat of armour . . . an armour that causes another kind of distance and compounds the problem yet again.

But we had that killing on Sunday night in Orlando; forty-nine people dead. Others in critical condition. I don't know what to say. It's so awful. The love that surfaces after such an atrocity is wonderful to see, but the hate and insecurity and rage and invisibility that caused it remain. So the answer to disenfranchisement these days, I guess, is to take as many people out with you, including yourself, as you exit in an imagined blaze of glory . . . that's the deal now. That's what you do. When I was a child in the 50s, we'd have these innocent and harmless private fantasies about people wishing they'd been nicer to us when they were all gathered at our funerals . . . but now, that's actually the case. That's the scenario. No fantasy.

The wind on my face this morning up at Mutrie with Mosey. The velvet touch of Mosey's head. The bright valley stretching out in greens. The sun. Texture. Why isn't it enough? Why isn't this gift of life enough? Where does the hate and greed take root? Why can't we locate it so we can fix it?

*Matins 25, June 22, 2016*

Talking about, or writing about parallel worlds is one thing. The idea is so fascinating and, all by itself, it offers an amalgam of possible redemption through the spectrum of variations it embodies. Start here. End up there. Or start there and end up here. Slight variations turn into major variations. Opening doors. Closing doors. You can see the appeal, the hope. But sometimes I feel another manifestation of the parallel worlds conundrum in my own life. And it's not science fiction. In one day I might step into six different ways I engage with the world. In each case, as I step into its texture and its face, I believe this is the most intense engagement I have and I believe in it completely. But later, moments later even, when I slide into the next version, I become convinced *that* it is the richest version, that I should put all my energy in it. In the end, every day, I simply move through these versions and that movement itself becomes my life, an infinitely changing intensity and texture and, even, shifting loyalties. Strange for sure, but sometimes very real. It makes life complex for spouses and friends for they get surprised a lot. They can even get fooled. But I'm not surprised. I'm never surprised.

*Matins 26, June 27, 2016*

Listening to Joe Lovano's "Welcome" on Steve Kuhn's CD, *Mostly Coltrane*. I need something this soft but solid today. Like a crazy prairie wind blowing in as a psychic blotter . . . soaking things up and away . . . yeah, just a crazy time lately . . . Jude's osteo-arthritis in her feet is so bad it causes a crisis, really, especially a crisis re: thinking about the future. And it's just the way it is. There is no blame, only a deep, almost profound sorrow and beneath it, I suspect, a hurt that is complicated and hard to explain . . . a hurt in Jude, and a hurt in me, too, for sure. A lesser hurt, but still there, still powerful.

No exit.

Just reinvention of the self & the world & the nature of joy and 'rush' . . . but every day, every morning . . . pretty damn exhausting . . . and yet, and yet . . . purposeful . . . and, in its own way, a unique kind of joy and celebration in itself . . .

*Matins 27, June 28, 2016*

*For Julia and Neil*

That sponge-like thud of the forest floor echoing up from beneath your feet, a dusky red and dove-grey, plumb richness of the forest floor that looks so solid but because you can hear and feel the thud of your feet you realise you are walking on something that is complex and hollow in places as well as solid, like a sponge must be. And though it has a dusty veneer over it, especially on hot days like this one, it is equally damp, buoyed up with moisture, again like a sponge. Walking forward over this puzzle, following my Welsh Springer Spaniel Mosey, sniffing my way to Bethlehem to be . . . I tell ya! One of those great, stretched mornings, aghast with sunlight and blue, soft in people whispering, cooing to their pets, lost on their ways, too. Found. This thicket of thinking and seeing and breathing and air being gulped in then out, in then out, a gift in this fragrance of leaves and bark and sunlight on moving water, my dog in and out of the rushing creek, taking more time in the shallows, smiling that goofy spaniel smile back at me, his tongue dangling almost a foot out of his mouth, he's so happy, his body in its element, in ecstasy . . . right back atcha Mosey! . . . William Stafford, meet Don McKay . . . Gwendolyn McEwen, meet this rushing water head on, you beautiful voice . . . Marshal McLuhan, meet Jake Kennedy . . . this puzzle . . . this ground we stand on . . . this sponge . . . we're always halfway there, always balancing . . .

*Matins 28, July 5, 2016*

Didn't get out for my trek with Mosey this morning . . . there's a fine, steady rain falling over everything and Mosey, being Mosey, would have been too dirty on our return . . . so we'll attempt it later . . . but I love the smell of rain here in this valley, in the mountains, so fragrant, so soft . . . it's different from the Prairie rains I grew up with . . . both beautiful, but different, too . . . different kinds of densities, different kinds of beauty . . . blah, blah, blah . . .

On Sunday I sat in the living room and watched Iceland play France in the Euro16 Quarter Final . . . Jude was out with her sister, so it was just me and Mosey . . . I knew everyone was openly or secretly cheering for Iceland . . . the team was so stunning and had upset everyone to get here . . . but France rolled over them, of course, 4 to zip by the end of the half. OK. OK. Typical. For a second I wished that my old Scottish friend Craig was sitting here with me watching this because sports was always a class thing with us . . . always loaded with mysterious, unaccountable metaphors for our own lives . . . we were always cheering for the working-class teams, the underdogs. And mostly losing . . . but still. Chicago. Pittsburg. Green Bay. Scotland. Regina. A strong, deliriously doomed pattern. But we loved it, of course, and the Iceland/France game was perfect for this . . .  but Craig's away . . . and the crazy thing in the second half is that Iceland wins the second half . . . not the game, but the second half . . . and their fans are so beautiful in honouring them that my eyes welled up as usual . . . I can't figure it out, but the older I get the more moving I find everything . . . it's ridiculous . . . pathetic . . . but there ya go! It's some old Yeats' mystery that has to do with life and art, life sort of winning, but not really . . . So there I sat, patting Mosey's head as the Iceland players clapped in unison up to their fans in the stands, and I found myself weeping for the crazy dignity and hope and righting of universal wrongs that this game had become for me . . . stranded in that zone of precarious non-definition, where no absolutes come in to save you, and instead, you realise you will always be suspended, turning, in this field of unresolved beauty, both creating and destroying itself with the same energies, the same persistent effort and striving . . . on some botched working-class raft that's sailing to Byzantium for sure . . . for sure . . .

When my dad retired from teaching, he was fifty-eight and they moved to Vernon for four years . . . it was a real adventure for them to move here, and a real risk, too . . . but both my parents were used to taking risks for us, so it was great really . . . I worried about Dad . . . now that he was retired, I worried that he might not make the effort to make new friends, engage with things, become too isolated in himself . . . he was such a bright and, I thought, social guy . . . and I'd drive up on certain Sundays and there he'd be in any season . . . watching a game by himself . . . it didn't matter to him . . . he loved hockey, American football, Canadian football, baseball, even golf . . . and, of course, because I was so young I didn't see it right . . . you know how it is . . . you never see it right in the moment . . . always and only later, afterward . . . but anyway, I'd be standing there looking at him, feeling sorry for him, imagining a different Dad with all sorts of friends and interests, and he'd look up at my silly solicitous and patronizing face and say, "What? WHAT? . . . Sit down! Relax!"

Dad passed away early, at sixty-nine. But he died at home in the middle of the night. Good karma.

It's my birthday in three days. I'm turning sixty-eight.

Exactly.

Almost like a postscript, last night they showed the Iceland Soccer Team arriving back in Iceland from France. It seemed and sounded like the whole damn country was there to cheer them on, and to thank them, and to honour them. Again, I was sitting by myself in the dark, loving it, and again, my eyes welled up.

I know I've got to get going. I need to write a few things, or, at least, try. I know I should reconnect with that art world. But this is so great, sitting here in the dark instead, suspended in this prism, delighting in every damn thing that happens, even Mosey turning his head slightly now, and looking right into me . . . all big things . . . even universals . . .

*What?*

*Matins 29, July 7, 2016*

The three of us out at the BX Dog Park this morning, Jude on her bike, Mosey confused, running back and forth, trying to be with both of us simultaneously . . . literally beside himself . . . the three of us in wonder, buoyant, successful . . . to see her out there in these elements, in her element, the way it should be . . . sometimes, the darker side of this rush is to feel like some wizened professional mourner, wailing my grief up into any cobalt sky that opens up at how unfair this has all been for this person, this love who is still a young, beautiful and hopeful woman . . . to have been dragged through so much in her body . . . and still be riding her smile out here over the blue and green meadows, her fierceness another breeze, another triumph of dust and rain and time . . . and there is no outlet for this anger . . . *I know that, I know that* . . . it must evaporate like water off stone . . . there is no blame . . . instead such grief must simply rise up and become its own element, invisible and now healing . . . *I know that, too* . . . but I still look for an outlet, a target sometimes, still clench my fists involuntarily, glaring . . . I'd be worried if I *didn't* . . . all part of a larger wheel, a matrix clock of greater logic that tumbles in an armature of steel and gold so perfect, so tempered it cannot be seen or measured . . . there . . . I've said it . . .

*Matins 30, August 17, 2016*

Just want to record this small quote from Kundera:

"A Person who is both an intruder and gentle is condemned, by an implacable logic, to apologize throughout his whole life."
— p 59, *The Festival of Insignificance*, Milan Kundera, Harper Collins, 2015

*Matins 31, September 27, 2016*

Just finished mowing the lawn. And I am tumbled out and over and into all that cut green, fragrant, photosynthesis of memory, repetition, repetition, walking through parallel/parallel worlds led by my nose. Pretty tactile. Braided. Almost real (why would I diminish it in that way?) Because it *was* almost real. That's why. But a concrete comfort nonetheless. Just the thought of all those John Lents walking over all that grass, walking through all those intersections in time. You bet. Jude feeling better today. It's going to be this day, then this day, then this day. That's the way it's going to be. And that's all right. She just needs to have a side-kick. We all do. Sometimes that's what my wish has been: that I might show up to be a side-kick for myself . . . pretty pathetic, but there you go. That's always the dark risk for people afflicted by a dysfunctional people-pleasing virus. Not something we set out to be infected by. Didn't plan on it. And maybe especially didn't see that cloak of martyrdom arriving, as always, just a bit too late to see it clearly. Ah well. Otherwise, all systems go. It's a beautiful day. Everything is happening at once. Whoosh! The whole mystery an endless contraction of the universe. That's how Jack Schratter calculated it years ago. I think he was right. Completely. There! Now. See? See.

*Matins 32, Wednesday, October 12, 2016*

So the smallest thing — wiping the countertop to the left of the stainless steel sink with a J-cloth, the J-cloth just freshly squeezed in a piping hot rinse — the smallest gesture becomes a celebration simply because you are *in* it, you are part of every thing, you are alive. And you've just realised that soon, in time, that might not be the case. So it's the pleasure, the dignity in each thing as it unfolds in the air, as it becomes its own architecture in time and space, as it becomes a molecular cathedral, like you . . . like you. And then nothing. You have to let it all roll forward at that point without you, something you also love the idea of because it is a part of love to understand the borders, the edges, the way things start and stop . . . a very big part of love.

*Matins 33, October 25, 2016*

Sun through the studio window . . . beautiful fall day full of maple leaves and sumac leaves and horse chestnut leaves all around us this morning, Mosey some quiet shadow slipping through any of these cross-hatching mysteries of gravity and buoyancy, both. Inside and out, eh? Perfect. Jake sent me an old NFB documentary on the Toronto Jazz scene 1961 and it is so powerful in the closeness of its black and white images, the clarity of the seemingly rough and improvised sounds. The movement of the documentary as it attempts to catch the movement of the music . . . so it's all movement and we return, again, to the shadowed cross-hatching gravity and buoyancy inside and outside, these scratched, contoured conte lines almost tattooed on my chest this morning morning morning morning mourning morning as old as these hills I guess, as obvious and as inaccessible until you do not fight the shadows, watching them, tracing them even, but become them as a natural thing in itself, suspended, alive, and dying in this studious light.

*Matins 34, November 29, 2016*

Finished Patti Smith's *M Train* this morning, in the middle of the night actually. 3:30 AM. Couldn't sleep. I'd had one of those days that won't let you go, when your whole being vibrates with either/ors that are impossible, inflated, but real. So there I was, then, looking for redemption and, by gum, finding it in Smith's beautiful meditations. There is, in her, a sacred kind of seeing or 'attesting to' or 'awareness of' caused by quiet observation — mostly of physical objects — that causes the internal world to perform a dance in the external world. That's what she does for me. It's embedded in her use of language, the awareness of how important sentences are to her, an incredible ear for syntax and the relationship — almost visceral in itself — between syntax and logic/meaning, an actual way of seeing . . . here are some small gems: (from the First Vintage Books Edition, 2016 . . . isbn 978-1-101-91016-0):

*"There were a lot of people in a hurry on the street, as if last-minute shoppers on Christmas Eve. I hadn't noticed at first and it seemed they were steadily multiplying. A young woman brushed past me with an armful of flowers. A dizzying perfume lingered, then dispelled, replaced by a vertiginous refrain. I felt conscious of everything: a beating heart, the scent of a song wafting in a conflict of breezes, and the human current heading home."* 141 ( . . . reminds me of Carver's 'Fat' and 'What We Talk About When We talk About Love'.)

*"I walked over and stood where he had been standing and felt the warmth of his presence. The wind was picking up and unidentifiable bits of debris were circling in the air. Something was coming, I could feel it."* 207/08 (again Carver, same as above.)

*"Images have their way of dissolving and then abruptly returning, pulling along the joy and pain attached to them like tin cans rattling from the back of an old-fashioned wedding vehicle."* 232

*"Now it's your song, I said, addressing a lingering void. The world seemed drained of wonder. I did not write poems in a fever."* 235

*"I believe in movement. I believe in that lighthearted balloon, the world. I believe in midnight and the hour of noon. But what else do I believe in? Sometimes everything. Sometimes nothing. It fluctuates like light flitting over a pond. I believe in life, which one day each of us will lose."* 249

*"I'm going to remember everything and then I'm going to write it all down."* 253

*"How can a writer place a living thing in the hands of the reader?"* 275

Matins 35, March 26, 2017

Was walking with Mosey up at the Grey Ditch Canal path off Rugg Road today, Jude waiting in the car because the osteoarthritis in her feet is so bad today, and Mosey and I are humping it up the hill about a half a mile in when this fragrance of wood burning — what kind of wood even, apple, spruce? — bolted me back directly to being in a car with two friends in the late spring in Edmonton, must have been seventeen or eighteen, driving a gravel road that rimmed all the cottages on Pigeon Lake on a Friday night, on the west side of the lake where the richer kids had summer cottages, and we could smell the scent of backyard fires burning through the open windows of the car, and we could hear the light, free sounds of young people our age laughing, and my heart was beating abruptly with all the sound and flesh and possibility of everything that was ever going to happen to me from that moment on and then, even then in that innocence, in the thick interstices of its fragrance, that burning, some part of me knew that all the conditions that contained these fragrances, these possibilities, would always and unconditionally apply so that even though my heart was full with an almost boundless surge of optimism in that moment in the car, the elation was contained and tempered by the conditions that had created and held it: the gravel road on the rim of beauty, the looking-in-on longing, the laughter and flesh that was rippling just beyond my reach . . . I would always be close and I would always hear and register the texture of it, but I would never be in it, or of it, or if by some accident I did end up in it momentarily, I would soon find myself kicked out and always looking back on it. That's just what was going to happen. Is that it? Is that it? Is that what all this is about? Even still?

I stop. I can see just the tip of Mosey disappearing behind a curve 100 yards ahead of me. It has been sunny enough today to dry the soft earth of the path and its dust rises up to compete with the fragrance of the burning wood in that orchard down there where I see two people pull up to the fire on an ATV, shrieking with laughter and excitement. I am closing in on it again. I am on its rim again. I can feel its heartbeat a few more hundred yards away down the path. That's where Mosey's headed, too. And I am also standing here crying in the dust and smoke. I'm not sure why, and I've never been more sure.

*Matins 36, Friday, May 12, 2017*

Three communities of images of pornography for scrutiny and meditation: actual trade pornography on the internet these days; archival footage of World War II atrocities before and after the war, and finally, the brutal but closely registered texture of a North American culture we are living out right now. I saw the James Baldwin documentary, *Not Your Negro*, tonight with Jude. Devastating to watch, but important in how it tries to face up to the complex contradictions in North American life, especially its undersides of violence, fear and hatred. Somehow, in my mind, there are huge connections between and among these three seemingly distinct and discreet communities of images. In juxtaposition, they tell a story we do not want to see or hear. It is a story about something big, a vast and dark longing that has never been admitted to or fulfilled in our culture. Let's think about that for a bit.

I remember my dad talking about James Baldwin. My dad lived near Harlem in 1950 and 1951. He listened to a lot of jazz in the clubs there. I was a two-year-old baby back in Antigonish, Nova Scotia, when he lived in New York and stared up into the night sky there, and stared down into those streets.

*Matins 37, May 25, 2017*

Jude and I out rolling through these East Hill streets on our bikes this morning. Wonderful. I get a visceral thrill sitting on that bike and it goes all the way back to Dad getting me that used three-speed at Allendale Hardware when I was eleven or twelve. How that felt. The rush of it. The imperfect red paint job on it. The stainless steel gears. The wind through my hair as I drifted down 109th Street north to the university district, or over Groat Road to the new Westmount Shopping Mall . . . the crazy independence of it, folding my arms in front of me, letting my legs do everything. Which they did automatically. That confidence that begins in an uncanny but abrupt adolescent awareness — only then, only then — of the subtlety of peripheral vision, then expands to include all hand and eye movement, the unconscious intricacy of the machinery that is built into you, that simply does everything. The confidence in your eyes and your feet, in your ability to balance things, pivot in the air, jump a low fence, leap across a small steam or big puddle. The body. Sacrament of wheels spinning in an almost imperceptible perpetual motion of undeclared ability. Our Lady of Perpetual Motion. Our Lady of hands and eyes. Our Lady of breath. Sacrament, yes. So Jake brought up Thomas Merton lately and that got me struggling through the early 60s again, through all those memories — but maybe especially, like Our Lady of Perpetual Motion, how my young fifteen-year-old consciousness — that untested bowl — spilled out and into those times, falling through the black and white images of *To Kill A Mockingbird*, *Lilies of the Fields*, *Breakfast At Tiffany's*, *A Man And A Woman*, *8 ½*, falling through those into my young ears listening to Odetta, Josh White, Phil Ochs, Tim Hardin, Ian & Sylvia, Gordon Lightfoot and Bob Dylan, into those and out that netting into the civil rights movement itself, all that slow, painful growth that required careful but brutal change, then through the equally careful but rich model of a thinker like Merton, through him and all that *other*, to be riding a bike through these suburbs now, these times, these equally post-war times . . . but what war are we lurching out of and into or away from now, these three-dimensional pains and after-images . . . what rough beast now . . . the great undoing of consciousness, the great collapse backward . . . I tell ya . . . but in another inevitable way, and from another angle, I know, or I hope I know, it is all yet another grand and necessary correction toward love . . . you just wait and see . . . I can sense it blossoming and billowing somewhere offstage, somewhere in the margins, peripheral . . . and I can sense it just as perfectly and confidently as my twelve-year-old body would have folded its arms defiantly on that three-speed, letting the legs balance everything, sensing all this exquisite perpetual motion machinery right smack dab in the middle of this body . . . *hoc test enim corpus meum* . . . a sacrament of peripheral vision, a perpetual Thomas Merton *mobile*, that sees everything you ever need to see . . . just you wait and see . . .

# Two

*And Its Accompanying Flywheel*

## Atomistic Plates: Your Father's Beat

*for Jake David Kennedy and his father, and Kevin McPherson Eckoff and his father, the constraints being: (a) the sizes of the six small fliers left on the table top at Hermann's Jazz Club on December 4, 2012, and (b) the Andrew Greenwood Quartet's tribute to Dexter Gordon billowing around me while I wrote on the clear white backs of those fliers.*

1.

My father's years in the b-bop zone were 1949 and 1950 in old New York New York, me a baby left behind in Antigonish, my dad rustling through the indigo night trumpeting side-streets scattering out like sound from Columbia University where he was a student completing his Master's Degree in literature and education . . . who did he hear? . . . what clubs? . . . A horn himself, my dad composing his life my life two blasts at the start of the tune that gets us here tonight: him dead for over twenty years now and me sixty-four sitting in Hermann's Jazz Club in Victoria, thinking of him first, and thinking of Dexter Gordon, too . . . my dad! . . . where do the emotions crack and squeak and billow out into the air in the face of that complex starting point, that simplicity of notes leaning heavily into the night sky Dexter Gordon's playing back to my dad and to me as visceral as the arborite beneath this flier I'm writing on, this old brown and orange 50s carpet I'm shuffling my boots on tonight as I did as a kid walking onto the posh broadloom in The Jubilee Auditorium in Edmonton the winter I turned fourteen in 1962 and I worked as an usher there so I could hear visiting musicians like Dave Brubeck play for free, my dad sleeping at home that night, sleeping it off: the whole composition we were writing our signatures on (our coda) on a thousand winter evenings lost in love? . . .

2.

*At the still point of the still turning at the fucking still point of the still fucking turning at the blessed still point of the still turning still turning still turning turning still so fucking still pointed turning of the point is still . . .*

3.

*Sanctus.*

4.

*That* is no country for old men . . . *OR* . . . *this* is no country for old men . . . *OR* . . . the young in one another's arms . . . *OR* . . . the birds in the trees; it just *IS* old men and the young and the birds and the trees and the fish, I tell ya, *sanctus* . . .

5.

. . . come back here you little fuck come back to the *sanctus* part you bet your late New York night it is every thing and turning still right now and in your face and I'm talking to *you* boy! *You! Listen!*

6.

. . . these young musicians are so beautiful tonight, Dad, playing their tribute to Dexter Gordon the way you blew your selves through the topaz charcoal notation of those New York nights so you could imagine me sitting here tonight — some big, fat lineage acoustic, safe in some ways, sure, but poised over all the endless edges you and I always precipiced over — but still playing it back for you anyway, this love . . . what else could we ever name it, this song we've braided together up into the blue air? . . .

7.

Bee-bop-a-loo-bop: *SHE'S MY BABY!*

Bee-bop-a-loo-bop: *I DON'T MEAN MAYBE!*

But I *do* mean maybe . . .

. . . I *do* . . .

. . . variable *sanctus,*

new whole . . .

*Atomistic Plates: Your Father's Beat*

When I wrote this poem in late 2012, I was down for a week in Victoria, BC, to be on a panel for the BC Arts Council's annual competitions and awards. One night I went down to Hermann's Jazz Club because they had mounted a tribute to Dexter Gordon who was such a pivotal part of the surfacing of bebop in New York city in the early 50s. Jay Ruzesky had told me about this event when we'd met for supper early in my stay. And because of my friendship with the poets Jake Kennedy and Kevin McPherson-Eckoff back in the Okanagan, I decided to write a poem for them about sitting and listening to this tribute to Dexter Gordon by implementing constraints . . . the kinds of Oulipian restraints both Jake and Kevin sometimes used in their own poems . . . just to see what might happen. It's a wonderful, risky way for me to set out to write something . . . a bit like throwing the dice, or improvising in jazz. And as it turned out, the evening itself offered me wonderful opportunities for restraints and improvisations. At each table in Hermann's there was a pile of small posters advertising the performance schedule and the individual performers who were booked to perform over the next stretch, through the holidays. So I flipped these small posters over and throughout the night, in conjunction with the songs being played and improvised, I wrote on the backs of them. The size of each poster was my constraint. A poem in seven parts emerged and not surprisingly, it focused on my dad who, as a young man of twenty-eight, had lived in New York city while attending Columbia University in 1949 and 1950 . . . at the birth of the bebop stage of jazz, when Dexter Gordon was playing in the clubs. My dad's favorite singer back then was Billie Holliday and he drifted into those clubs and listened to her. When I got back to Vernon from Victoria, I kept working on this compressed little poem and eventually, about ten months later, I gave both Jake and Kevin copies of it along with copies of the original constraint posters and the handwriting on the backs of them plus a cover page I had drawn for them for fun. I have included everything here because there is still something fascinating about how and when this material surfaced, maybe especially because I had a heart attack three weeks after writing this poem in Hermann's, and here I am now, five years later, as healthy as a horse, and here, too, is the poem in all its lumps and imperfections as well . . .

*Outside the Sylvia (1986)*

monolithic logs heave and interrupt the beach
every fifteen seconds a jogger in bright clothes carries
the sand to the sky somewhere nearer Stanley Park
Beach Avenue rattles its supper traffic

gargantuan elms oversee these
their branches scratch at the low soup sky
fracture the soft distances of the bay

farther down the street
next to a flashing red traffic light
are the forest green awnings of an
expensive restaurant

pastel apartments hunch and hover in the wind
crowd the quilted patches of green grass and
the many-coloured people switching over them

everything is in motion

the skyline Kitsilano

as I look away
fifty seagulls implode
a collapsing beige umbrella
on a middle-aged woman's hand
flinging birdseed onto the sand

then the seagulls depart
umbrellas unfurl everywhere

all the car lights switch on beneath
the green awning and the traffic light

only the sea is still and even it is

still moving

*Outside the Sylvia, Again (2016)*

*For Jude May Clarke*
*(And for Jake David Kennedy's notion of 'being at the table' and how hard he made me think about that)*

"The thing that is lost in this kind of thinking, the kind that proposes a 'moment' in which religion is freed by 'hermeneuticization,' is the self, the solitary, perceiving, and interpreting locus of anything that can be called experience[ . . . ]subjectivity is the ancient haunt of piety and reverence and long, long thoughts. And the literatures that would dispel such things refuse to acknowledge subjectivity, perhaps because inability has evolved into principle and method."

— Marilynne Robinson, *Absence of Mind*, 2010

"This law [Beethoven's final rights of the aesthetic] is revealed precisely in the thought of death . . . Death is imposed only on created beings, not on works of art, and thus it has appeared in art only in a refracted mode, as allegory . . . The power of subjectivity in the late works of art is the irascible gesture with which it takes leave of the works themselves. It breaks their bonds, not in order to express itself, but in order, expressionless, to cast off the appearance of art. Of the works themselves, it leaves only fragments behind, and communicates itself, like a cipher, only through the blank spaces from which it has disengaged itself."

— Theodore Adorno, "Late Style in Beethoven," in *Essays on Music*, ed. Richard Leppert, 2002

> *"He does not know yet that for those of his class and condition, born close to the earth and quick to fall back to it once again [ . . . ] he was a peasant. We will never learn how he suffered, in what circumstances he was made ridiculous, the name of the café where he got drunk [ . . . ] . . . [A]s with all so-called upstarts who cannot make others forget their origins any more than they can themselves, who remain poor men exiled among the rich without hope of return [ . . . ]"*
>
> — Pierre Michon, "The Life of Andre Dufourneau," *Small Lives*, trans. Jody Gladding and Elizabeth Deshays, (1984) 2008.

. . . a Starbucks on Denman and Davie, looking out on English Bay, just south of The Sylvia where we're staying for two nights. She's asleep right now. It's late afternoon. Seagulls swell everywhere overhead like sheep in Scotland . . . ubiquitous in the winds and sunlight, wild in any eye today, almost unusual in early February . . . and out in the bay eleven freighters, their bright-orange hulls bobbing high in the water: empty, waiting . . .

. . . and here I sit, thirty years later, looking out at the same visual field, but everything has changed, of course, especially me. I am sixty-five now, not thirty-five, and my heart, though full of longing, is not the restless, buzz-seeking heart I lived through back then, always needing a hit, a surprise, not always movement exactly, but things in metamorphosis . . . sure . . . that's the thing about being young . . . maybe it's part of the physiological imperative to increase and multiply . . . to breed through movement, friction, moisture . . . OK . . . all right . . . speaking of which movement, wonderful women walk by in the street, the full spectrum, a wide representation matching all the selves I am sitting here watching them through . . . it's the same mystery I wrote about in 1984 in a poem written exactly here, called "Outside the Sylvia" — it's the same perpetual motion machine of mutability — but *I* am different in it . . . my sense of the music is different (what if Edward Said and Theodore Adorno were both *wrong* about what they envisioned as 'late style'? . . . and instead of it being a collapse, a failure, a fragmented descent into an inchoate chaos, it was, instead, a last gate into a new kind of formless beauty, not executed by conventional 'laws' . . . what then?) . . . yes, my sense of this music is different, especially after the events of this last year . . . I can see, sometimes, a thick blackness overtaking me . . . I don't even know how to put it into words . . . it's not a game . . . it's not an enchantment with image or metaphor . . . it is a glimpse of the state of not being at all, and it doesn't look like an ocean to me, something crossed . . . how is that possible? . . . what might Yeats say? Talk about change or metamorphosis . . . what bird might he imagine to get him out of this one?

That is no country for old men

    This is exactly the field I need

        The young in one another's arms

            The old in one another's arms

                Birds in the trees, those birds

                    in the trees all of us all winter

                        long, caught in that sensual

                  music we can't neglect, forget

              monuments of un-ageing intellect

            and become, instead, the flesh

        and blood-mire birds we

    actually *are* . . . give it up . . . give

it up . . .

. . . so in the face of the nearness of that forest — why forest? — I want to race through these meadows now — why meadows? — over this grass — what grass? — my lungs full and my heart beating out its life here in the fire — why fire? — and her, my life's love — whatever that means and it means a lot, believe me — this adjacent grail of skin, here with me now, down here to wrestle with her kidneys after thirty years of lupus . . . there, I've said it . . . it's always that kind of table, isn't it, Jake? . . . it's what we know and even love, though we often wish it wasn't so familiar, the *kind* of table, that is . . . we sometimes are tricked into thinking it might be some *other* kind of table which we'd never love or feel comfortable with anyway . . . and she and I have been down here many times before, facing other health crises . . . this one seems the fiercest, but we'll see . . . she's still smiling in the face of it and, again, it's not a small thing to face . . . it's not some sentimental TV movie where everything's going to be just fine in the end . . . it's none of that . . . but it *is* this table here *right now*, and this window and my own winter boots shuffling on the floor beneath me, and English Bay spreading itself out around me, its afternoon asphalt traffic surging in a permanently white-noised arrested gesture of anticipation and hope — *almost there, almost arriving; almost there, almost arriving* — and you bet I'm sitting here, finally, empty in the best way, drained and full, without design, not a metaphor in sight . . . *well* . . . or, as Walker Percy's crazy, wonderful Will Barrett might say, "WAIT A MINUTE!" . . . what *about* those freighters . . . *come on now . . . admit it . . . just look at them!* . . . their buoyant bright orange hulls bobbing on a blinding Byzantine blue.

*Have Yourself A Merry Little Christmas . . . (2002)*

I heard the story of the writing of this old classic this morning on CBC Radio. Judy Garland, the leading lady of *Meet Me in St, Louis*, (1944) twenty years old herself, was worried there was too much melancholy attached to her film personae, so she wanted the slightly sad, initial lyrics to this song changed, made more upbeat. This was a revelation to me as I'd always heard the song as a sad, almost sarcastic piece in places. But that was just me, likely, though I do think a melancholy stays with the piece if only through its music.

I'm in the throes of Christmas shopping today and all the usual soft blues that accompany that. All the triple-thinking, quadruple-thinking, guilt, questions, regrets, nameless sorrows, even rages that accompany my knowing the world is so unfair, so fucked up, so out of whack, that to be in the middle of a buying frenzy, no matter how modest or well-intentioned, even touching, raises a spectrum of almost infinitely recessive compromises. You know how it is. You can sit in your living room complaining that the economic scale has gone completely mad because you're making $60,000 a year and a hockey player is making ten million, a baseball player just signed a seven-year deal for 135 million. And you're sitting there watching your colour TV to get this very information, gnawing on a Snickers Bar maybe, or smelling the pork roast cooking somewhere, off in the distance of the kitchen, halfway through its cooking so the smells of roast have overtaken the house with promise. And it occurs to you suddenly that some person in Botswana is imagining you thinking of the baseball player, and some other person in Afghanistan is imagining the person in Botswana imagining you, and so forth . . . And in each case you sense a different way in which all things are out of scale until/unless everyone is safe, until/unless each person is eating, until/unless everyone is reading, until/unless everyone is free, and the impossibility of these layers of striving becomes a thought as overwhelming as the thought of infinity and you give in to the bigness of it because you don't know what to do otherwise. And finally, the upbeat/downbeat contradictions in the song that started this train of logic make more sense in its sweet sadness, its triumph and its quiet undertow of sorrow, and your eyes well up in a nameless flood of longing and gratitude.

Then I make the enormous mistake of picking up the December 20 issue of *The New York Review of Books* and open it to an article written by Charles Simic on two new books that have come out by Czeslaw Milosz. And the opening parapgraph reads thus:

> "*'They wrote as if history had little to do with them' — that's how I imagine some future study of American poetry describing the work of our poets in the waning years of the twentieth century. Like millions of their fellow citizens, they believed they could, most of the time, shut their eyes to the world, busy themselves with their lives, and not give much thought to evil. A hermetic literary culture, Czeslaw Milosz would say, is a cage in which one spends all one's time chasing one's own tail. To realize from one's own experience that there's nothing, no matter how vile, that human beings will not do to one another was until recently a knowledge reserved for the thousands of immigrants whose life stories, had they been able to make sense of them, would have still sounded farfetched and incoherent. Anyone who lived through and survived the many horrors of the last century found himself with an experience nearly incommunicable to someone who still had faith in the basic goodness of man.*"
>
> — Charles Simic, "A World Gone Up in Smoke," *The New York Review of Books*, December 20, 2001 (Volume XLVIII, Number 20).

So I'm sitting there, caught in my sense of the meanness of my own times, humbled even more if I run those times against any international standard — even when I weigh in the new, right-wing, mean-spiritedness and small-souled bottom lines of Klein, Harris and, now, here in my province, Gordon Campbell — when abruptly I am forced to consider that I write outside of my own history. The implication of Simic's attack is clear: if he or she is not careful, the average North American writer is creating outside history, "as if History had little to do with them". And then, just to cinch the downward spiral of a deal I must have cut with the universe this fall, I stumble onto Andrew O'Hagan's review of Franzen's *The Corrections* in the December 13th issue of *The London Review of Books*. In a stage-managed, weary tone, O'Hagan begins:

> "Today there are only second acts in American lives. No generation to find itself interestingly lost in Paris; no elegant tribe crowding the lawn with portents of disaster

*at Gatsby's parties; no collective urge to write the great war novel; no second sex. To judge by the best of the new writing, the most urgent of the new films, the most watched television, American lives are now devoted to a wholesale inhabiting of the dead afternoon. It is not the world of beginnings nor the world of ends that obsesses: it is what Lionel Trilling called the middle of the journey. There is limbo, there is stasis, there is open-all-hours petrification. There is mild domestic psychosis and there are soft furnishings. All arty is the art of real estate and self-help. The universe described is a middle-class America, a place of spiritual lassitude and window-blinds. Market populism travels in through the air-conditioning and fastens to the red blood cells. And in these lives, and in the books and films that venture to look at these lives, you notice how a single, powerful question pertains: what now?*

Again, the implications are clear. All the soft echoes of Eliot, the psychological and historical contexts O'Hagan needs to tackle the texture of Franzen's novel, are understandable. Now, I have to tell you I am a fan of Simic and Milosz; and an even more natural fan of O'Hagan, especially his book *Our Fathers*. But the implications, *especially* reinforced by the echoes of Eliot, seem, again, unforgiveable, even sloppy. O'Hagan is trying to simplify American writing, trying to name a new decade by raising the previous simplifications drawn to account for American modernism in fiction. A journalist looking for the next best thing, a new fix, a textual sound bite to solve a temporary, short-term problem: his dislike of a new book. What did Kundera say back in that 1984 Granta interview with McEwen about that danger in journalism, its "fast thinking"?

Here's the deal, and both Milosz and O'Hagan seem to miss it entirely. It's the old forest for the trees conundrum. As a Canadian writer of fiction and poetry, and as obscure and regionalized as the reach of my own six books has been, I am writing out the heart of what I am trying to articulate. I am not making sweeping statements about middle-class life or the heartland of North American life because I both live that life and occupy it. But the conundrum, the deal, is this: North America actually *is* the great social and political experiment of the last three hundred years. It is easy for *anyone* to look down any kind of refined imperial nose to criticize this experiment. So many parts of it have gone badly. It's *true*. But, from my point of view, sitting here in this small city in the interior of British Columbia, in this high valley in the mountains, listening to Judy Garland sing "Have Yourself A Merry Little Christmas", it seems to me we've had enough action of the kind Wyndham Lewis used to parody in his novels in the 30s. We've had enough kinesis. So what about this stasis, this petrification, what O'Hagan refers to — and I keep thinking of Richard Ford's use of this word in his astonishing novel, *Wildlife* — limbo? What kind of territory or war is it, or to hearken back to Milosz' comments — what kind of contemporary *history* is it ? Not a ravaged European landscape — what Sylvia Plath referred to as "wars, wars, wars" but the territory of subjectivity, of the interior, of what seems to be, from one point of view at least, stillness. *The dead afternoon*. Precisely where most political revolutions *lead* us, after all is said and done, but a condition or territory or struggle which few of us are prepared to survive. That's what fascinates me about the depth of the 'ordinary': not just the predictable, retro quality of the ordinary that burnishes itself through the dazzling mirrors of postmodernist/post-structuralist theory — all that soft pornography — but the terror of it, the heart of its darkness but the real *heart*, the real *darkness*: Ford's limbo. It was never Fitzgerald's overly-designed, pathetically forced 'green lights', never Hemingway's self-conscious bombast . . . he couldn't survive the stasis I'm thinking of . . . it was always Faulkner's ability to 'endure'. Not the gay emigrees and all the romantic self-destruction there, but, instead, where Eliot himself ventured in "Gerontion", "Preludes", "The Waste Land", "The Four Quartets". I'm glad the writers I admire go into this territory, this history. It's the most important war being fought right now, this battle for self-understanding: awareness. All revolutions approach it sooner or later, after the action, the medals, the applause. The dead afternoon that terrified poor old Prufrock, kept him pinned, petrified. Hopefully, aside from the success or lack of success in achieving it as in the case of Franzen and others, that's what this 'ordinariness' is about, a different way of engaging in history. A different war with different front lines.

And, finally, after all my own bombast here, I must return to the thought of Judy Garland singing that song in that cheesy old forties musical, made in the middle of World War Two, made as an inept attempt, likely, to cheer people up by reminding them of the promise of the twentieth-century incarnate in The World Fair it celebrates in St, Louis: that endlessly compromised, endlessly contradictory, but endlessly striving 'ordinariness', an ordinariness and stillness and afternoon that Marjorie Perloff locates and examines in her book, *Wittgenstein's Ladder: Poetic Language and the Strangeness of the Ordinary*. Both Simic & O'Hagen should take a close look at it.

*Atticus Riff (07/06/12)*

Watched *To Kill a Mockingbird* last night up at Betty's with Betty, Mary, Jo-Anne, Len, Sharon & Jude. Interesting, complicated grouping of cultural contexts absorbing this movie. All the live layers that spiral back to 1921. Traces of everything watching, and a concentrated trace being delivered in the movie itself. All of us suspended in the moral whirlpool the movie dramatizes. The ignorance, poverty, fear, and hatred on the one hand — especially the inheritance of civil war wounds, and the lingering sense (that Flannery O'Connor always wrestled with) that Yankees were smart-assed liberal know-it-alls who spent most of their free time (when they weren't reading books) passing judgement on the clodhopper south. But the beauty of Harper Lee's vision and the incredible empathy in the story still astonishes me. The only way to go, no matter how painful. Even Atticus admitting, in the trial, that he was not being idealistic about the final refuge of the American courts, but that he felt those courts were a real, living thing that insisted all people were created equal. That *To Kill a Mockingbird* — like Munro's *Lives of Girls and Women*, Ford's *Wildlife*, Mitchell's *Who Has Seen the Wind*, Joyce's *Portrait* — was a *bildungsroman*. Novel of development. Microcosm for how the self grows and is shaped. Augustine. Rousseau. Goethe. DeQuincey, Dickens, Butler, Lawrence, Lowry, Miller, Durrell . . . .and on and on. *New Waterford Girl. The Kiln. The Prowler.* Eileen Myles' *Inferno.* Same story, same story, same story. Always the same, no matter the shifting contexts, no matter what we might even see as 'progress'. The same story that needs to be told again and again, that we cannot see when it's happening . . . only and always after. Always the after-image. Powerful stuff. Complex template, syntax, grammar. Narrative. Conrad Aiken's *Ushant*, Lowry's *Ultramarine*. Proust. Necessary light.

## All the Wrong People Are Going to Live Forever

And it's going to be only too true. I keep thinking, when it seems funny, of that great short story by Flannery O'Connor, "Revelation", in which the beleaguered Mrs. Turpin rejects heaven in the final scene. In that scene, she is hosing down the hog barn, fresh from the doctor's office where the young neurotic girl from New York had called her a warthog from hell and had thrown the book at her, and she raises her head to the skies and has a vision of a heaven into which all people walk, including 'negroes' and 'white trash', and so flabbergasted is Mrs. Turpin by this egalitarianism, that she turns down heaven and its God on a matter of taste. She might have been quite interested in what the new frontiers of genetics and cloning and organ harvesting and the wide spectrum of human transplant medicine is beginning to offer in terms of eternal or extended life right here: a heaven of her own, rather than God's design.

Yes, the ultimate dream of capitalism: the sale of eternity to the folks with the money. The selling of, first, the body in all its parts to one set of humans who have the money, and second, for those who don't have the money, a lucrative opportunity to trade off eternity for more short-term gains by selling their organs or bodies to the first set with the money. Now, there's a two-tier system if I ever heard of one. Think of the possibilities.

But, as the Chinese say, "May you live in interesting times." Or its variation, "Be careful what you wish for." Even as far back as the Greeks, there's Tithonis achieving an eternity that is, at the least, a questionable achievement.

And all this based on the linear dream of longevity, as opposed to the circular dream of the richness of this life, here, now. I don't know. We've got it all wrong. We are not stopping long enough in this ecstasy of the technical to consult the philosophers who devote time to these issues. We'd better give them a call soon.

When it doesn't seem funny, I see an Hieronymous Bosch painting of a future in which bodies are harvested to serve the wealthy and the wealthy and privileged live forever in some kind of extended machinery of pleasure, of buying and selling, of appropriating everything from the flesh to the spiritual even, possibly some machinery of regret built into it, but always too late, always after the slaughter. Heaven help us.

(When I was younger and I stumbled into openings like this, I was conditioned to ignore them, dismiss them. The logic of that conditioning had a lot to do with the humility of being a student and understanding that the more I looked into things, the more complicated they became, and, as a consequence, the more I naturally imagined that minds greater than mine, certainly, were wrestling with these things and articulating them on a level I was not able to attain. The older I have become, however, the more I realize how inaccurate that humility can be sometimes, as healthy as it might be in other ways. What I discovered, I think — and I admit it's fleeting, my sighting of this next idea — but what I discovered is that each generation has a very narrow window of opportunity to move things forward — as small as a two- or three-year span — in which its matrix of fresh, new ideas/logic/ideological variations surface and then are simply paid attention to, pursued or forgotten in the rush of life, distractions, and all the other struggles that shuffle in to overwhelm us. It's over very quickly. The further realization is that it's not always a good thing to defer the ideas you stumble into; they may be gifts that surface from very hard work; they may be openings that are legitimate and you've just happened to stumble into one or two of them accidentally. It's not always a good thing to keep quiet about them. They may be important; they might save somebody else some trouble.)

*Hat Trick: Impossible Subjects (Democracy/ Philosophy/ Love)*
   *for Robert Kroetsch*

1. D E M O C R A C Y

Walking down 25th Street this morning in the sun and the quiet — it *being* Sunday morning — and the air lush with lilacs because it's their week this week, just like it is every early May. So I'm walking along the street and the lilacs make me think of the south side of Edmonton in the 50s, just after the war, when I was a kid going to school for the first time in 1954 and then, *even then*, my child's head would register a sweet, almost too-much-ness of the lilacs in the spring on the side roads where they coughed up their decadent, heavy artillery over the crushed gravel lanes and broken down back-alley fences, and I'm thinking this morning, exactly fifty-six years later, that the reason there are so many lilacs — even *now*, here in Vernon — is and always *was* because they didn't cost much . . . they were easy to get and to seed . . . they were sturdy green shrubs the rest of the year, and on top of such serviceability, they also had this miraculous, over-the-top beauty for at least a week in May. A bonus, for sure. So what a great, abundant, resilient beauty, I tell ya! My childhood was so thick in lilac — in about a thousand different ways — I may be a lilac myself. I wouldn't mind that one bit. Sturdy. Serviceable. Maybe over-the-top for one small stretch in a rhythm from time to time, the rest of the time just quietly there. Green. Part of the fabric. Nothing wrong with that. Humming away. Planted out on the edge of things, the periphery. Almost marking those edges or borders. Sure. Both enclosing and separating things. All right. OK. Supportive. Not too brassy. Fine.

And then this camper van begins to slide by me slowly on the street. It's the usual old half-ton camper van, made here in the Okanagan. Made just after the time I'm thinking of in Edmonton. It trundles by me this morning, heading south, and looks to have been made in the early 60s . . . I'd say about 1963. And as I watch it being carried away in the blue half-ton it's grown out of, I wonder, randomly at first, the way you *do* in the morning when you're just heading out into things and you don't have much to say, that kind of mood, I wonder about the history of camper vans, and I'm struck immediately by the exponential proliferation of them since the early 60s in North America. And as I watch the van signal right to head west on 39th Avenue, I think, for the second time this morning, well, yeah! *of course* they proliferated. They were easy to get or make. They were accessible. Everybody could get his or her hands on one and all these families could head out to beaches and campgrounds and favourite fishing lakes on the prairies or forests and waterfalls in BC, and pack up their food and their beer and their children and their sleeping bags and Coleman stoves and propane lanterns and checkered tablecloths and get away for a while, lurching innocently and happily into all the imperfections and contradictions built into what we imagined and realised as vacations back then. [To vacate something? Is that the root? Or some twist on 'calling', Vocation? That one doesn't sound right to me. In the French, *vacances*. I'll have to look it up. But who cares?] except anyway . . . what I *meant* to say was that these camper vans were absolutely wonderful. Accessible. Reliable. Not very mysterious, but each one completely original. Floating families, heading out, mobile, a kind of freedom. Not perfect, but nothing to be sneezed at or looked down upon either.

So the lilacs and the camper vans, after years of struggling and work, are able to set things up so their grandchildren can get what they've never been able to offer them: an education with all the sophistication and other classy side-effects that come with it. And just as these new lilacs and camper vans get to actually *go* to classes, some people decide to ramp up the usual walls of exclusivity built around knowledge and consciousness so that they are even *more* diabolical than they *ever* were, and a whole generation of lilacs and camper vans are taught how to *understand* lilacs and camper vans *for the first time* and they learn how to try to help them *save* themselves *from* themselves, and these grandchildren who are, at first, puzzled and a bit confused by the machinery of this new logic that has altered what they expected from their education, eventually give in — who wouldn't? — and find themselves learning to chuckle at the quaintness and modesty of lilacs and camper vans, then at the validity of lilacs and camper vans, then at the dysfunctional and limited *lives* of lilacs and camper vans, and so on as on The Quaker Oats Cereal Box, and in the end they acquire, *of course*, a rather mysterious, but generally patronizing *view* of lilacs and camper vans, so much so that one of these grandchildren — we'll call her Beatrice — why not, eh? — is walking through a dark wood in the middle of her life one morning, almost lost, when she sees, in a field to the left of the gravel road she's walking on north of Heisler, Alberta, that there is a rusting old camper van, red and white, abandoned and leaning against a grove of bright, burgundy lilacs in a farmer's field and she wonders, vaguely at first, well that's the *haystack* . . . this is trickster territory after all . . . and I'm the *needle* for heaven's sake . . . won't you just *look* at the wonderful origin of me staring right back at myself on this wonderful spring Sunday morning in my comedy, right in the middle of my comedy for fuck's sake, and I fucking *love* those lilacs and that van, and I'm going to stay here forever until my eyes fill up with darkness, and lilacs grow out of my ears and the radio in the camper van is playing "Your Cheating Heart" by Hank Williams over and over again and when I leave this world in time I will feel this crazy blessing here in the starting place, the ending place, all these crazy contradictions — sure, you bet, I'm not denying *any* of them — and I know, or I hope I know that there's going to be, there *will* be more respect in the world soon . . .

## 2. PHILOSOPHY: TRIPTYCH
*For Fiona Tan*

*One*

The evening grosbeaks pig out on
black-oiled sunflower seeds in front of
the window behind which my face sits
in a chair, this glass separating us.
The glass here in my house is a twelve-foot
wide series of windows with levered
openings onto screens and, finally, the air itself.
But that other glass, I'm not as sure about.
As natural as breath. Instinct.
Maybe it is constituted of breath and instinct.
I don't know. If I move my head, though,
even slightly, the birds panic, flit
up into that vault which is also
another *kind* of vault. If I keep
still I can be as close as
the glass allows.

There is always a membrane between us.

And a vault we collapse up into, too,
that whooshes us up into an exhilaration
that can almost kill us both.

My feathers twitch.

My talons scratch at the carpet.

*Two*

Sitting in a Starbucks on 4th Avenue
just west of MacDonald, the rain
a sheet of stumbling Tuesday colour.
Grey and mint-green and dark charcoal mirrors
of asphalt rolling by like something sure.

I don't know.

I am agonizing over a piece I wrote
that might have been misinterpreted;
read, in fact, in the exact opposite
direction of where I thought it was
going, and the thing is, *the thing is,*
I can read it the wrong way too,
and it makes perfect sense.

Holy crap. Literally. But it
actually *does* matter to me.

The problem is that, like the rolling,
mirrored asphalt carrying cars away to
somewhere sure, you could read
this piece I'm thinking about
and think I was against
education, and, having given my
whole life to that, believe me, that's
not what I intended. *What I intended*
was to warn myself and anyone else
who cares to listen that we have to be
cautious when we think we're trying to save
the world by rescuing people from
themselves. We just have to be extra

careful about the process, and if
the process requires an opening up
and questioning of everything, we
have to be sure we place *ourselves*
— all *our* imperfections and contra-
dictions — at the centre of that
*everything*. Otherwise we
make a mistake most revolutions
have made before us. That's all.
Simple.

If we allow contemporary philosophy
to atrophy into dogma — that we feel smug
and self-congratulatory about *because* of its
exclusions — we're already too late
to apply it. We've missed its
boat, and it will sail on
without us. In fact, it's
gone now. I saw it
leave.

I heard its creaking sails over
the sound of this traffic,
these sheets of rain.

Vanishing into tricky, open water.

*Three*

How many years have we done this?
Staying in a hotel room in Vancouver?
Down to hear a specialist interpret
the test results we've come down
with, so relieved when we navigate

all these swells and fades
of your body and its old,
dark side-kick, this crazy,
wise-cracking, Sancho Panza of a
chronic disease you were given
to wrestle with like an Old
Testament prophet arm-wrestling
an angel.

My arm falls over your naked silk hips
twelve stories above the sea gulls
trolling for garbage down on Burrard.
The wondrous flesh on flesh with you
for thirty-five years now.

What beauty you are!

And sometimes, in moments like this one,
*because* of you, no separation between
the thing and the thing itself.

That is the case sometimes.

## 3. LOVE: A DEAD SPARROW

At first I registered its body out
of the corner of my eye, the way
you do, its flat eyes open, dry disc
stones staring up into the sun on
the deck. I approached where it
had fallen from the Manitoba maple
and got down on my knees to
look at it: a sparrow, young,
neck broken, twisted to the side,
otherwise perfect. For some
reason I breathed on it, ruffling
its feathers in a soft transit,
then stared at its body, picked
it up, cupping it on the open
skin of both hands. I could see
and feel the death now and it
was too much — who knows
how these things happen
sideways on us like this
on unpredictable mornings,
coffee waiting in the kitchen
behind us — but it was too much,
and I didn't know why. I began
to weep over the body and
I raised it up into the morning
which was cranking itself up
and over the asphalt roofs
east down the back alley
behind the house. I held it
into the sun, then dropped

on my knees again, still cupping
the small dead weight, thinking:
*that's me that has fallen, that*
*has overreached the precision*
*of stairs in the sky, the*
*confidence of air. That's*
*me that misread everything and*
*has fallen so far into such*
*stillness. And that's me*
*holding me, too.* That's the
way it always is when the
best part of me mourns the
ritual deaths flown by the
other parts of me that never
quite get it right. And I knelt
there sobbing for this piston
life out here in the height
of air and sun, the dark
earth grinning back up —
me sobbing for this piston and
exulting in it, too, knowing
this small being had risked
everything to be loved
like this, cradled by such
attention, over and
over again, these
errors in physics, this
misread buoyancy:
risking everything
and often falling into
the complete darkness
of hands.

*Prague Spring: A Quartet from 'Prague Spring: Twelve Cubist Sonnets,'* 2008
   *For Terry Donnelly*

1

When you set forth in words like this, it's not as if you *will* the words to a final logic so the words become a simulacrum of something — the way a photograph seems to stop time, or a portrait copies part of something.

It's that you trust the words, like music, by starting out in the earth ground of the body, in the concrete field the body is registering around itself, will move into both the body and that electrical field around it, and by some bizarre circuitry, reach beyond both to that other matrix that is also there, that resists ordinary logic, that rushes the heart and the mind and surprises both, and is as close as we can get to saying what the breath of being is.

So it's not that the words copy.

They are set forth babbling, as probe.

They find things. They open things up. They become something.

[ . . . the young woman feeling sorry for me in the bakery earlier, forgiving me my awkward lack of confidence in *her* words, *her* language, and grinning at me so generously beyond both sets of words, she restored me to the bakery, pulled me back into my body standing in front of her from a point of view that was from farther on down the line, when I was already looking *back* at this moment and making fun of myself in it, full of swagger of course, the *traveller*. The *raconteur*. She rescues me from that and insists on placing me here, now, in *this* garden, my feet on the ground, her many gestures a cubist blessing from all sides simultaneously. Who would have thought that when I was starting out here? This is no trip into the ordinary . . . ]

2

That's what happens, maybe, when you ease into your 60s: you begin to see more. I just saw this man in his 70s — all dressed up, likely headed to the bank, looking pretty spiffy. He was walking along the street opposite the window I'm staring through in this coffee shop I've found at the corner of Kosi and Kolkovne in the old Jewish Quarter of Prague. He was checking his pants for something, doing something he was certain of. Then, abruptly, he stopped walking and, instead, stared up at the sky for no reason. He spotted something of interest up there and he began to squint at it, shading his eyes with his right hand on his forehead, stretching his mouth out wide in the process as if it might help the concentration, staring up at whatever it was. People just kept milling past him in a wild flow. Life went on. But he'd interrupted himself looking at something. Maybe for the first time. It's possible.

Of course, I was watching *him*.

And you?

That's what it feels like. Being a kid again. Seeing things for the first time. Watching the physics of the world around you disclose itself law for law, surface for surface, wheel for interlocking wheel.

Like the circular, waxed cardboard seals on glass milk bottles back in the 50s in Edmonton. The bottle was left on your front doorstep by the delivery man who drove a square, yellow van. In the winter the bottles would crack open in the cold if you didn't bring them in as soon as they were delivered, and the first thing to give was the circular cardboard seal. It'd be staring up at you at an odd angle supported by a churn of frozen milk that looked chalky and spongy. Some days, there'd be a glass bottle of chocolate milk there, too, and you'd all go crazy! What a surprise!

Before plastic.

Before franchises.

Before everything was processed.

Before you stopped seeing.

*Look! Here! It's spring!*

Bridal wreath is breaking out everywhere behind these stone walls. It's as if everything around you has been imagined by Derain and in the snap of two fingers, has become three-dimensional.

It's Prague!

Pivot!

3

I love each of my brothers and sisters. Four brothers, two sisters. We grew up in a fierce bond that cannot be broken, but our adult lives, and our different abilities to survive and enjoy them, are each of them unique, and, as a result, sometimes each of us feels perpetually stranded, each one of us looking for phantom limbs. And they're out there, those limbs. We must not forget that. They're out there intensely, and they whirl in a perpetual motion matrix that is always unfolding as the past, where love was first discovered, and where it was unconditional. The fact that we have been carried by these waters away from one another — into other loves and other families — is a sea that surrounds the first matrix, but doesn't alter it. These two oceans whirl, counter-clockwise, one around the other, alternating their movements like a beneficent, poised machine, some medieval clock clicking and clacking its way through the mornings, afternoons and evenings of our small delights and sorrows and, throughout it all, separated islands of recognition and affection. *If it could only* be *like this! If words could simply crack open these riddles sometimes and be the balm of love, its core.*

Hey, it's spring in Prague. I love each and every one of you. We will love one another beyond the dark carbon kiss that will lay each one of us down to rest eventually in the earth — all the double machinery and water in those moments seeming to caterwaul and collapse into another kind of dust, too — even then, and beyond what seems a ruined landscape of objects that are suddenly only partial things, reverberating beyond that even into another physics: an impossible poem that must reach out beyond itself, admitting everything, to be possible.

4

So you get, finally, to love. The texture of love in this strange, new city with her, this baroque, art nouveau, cubist dream of a city that seems to possess the familiarity that dreams have, that Kafka-esque tableau wherein you accept everything: of *course* this is Prague and I'm *in* it. Of *course*. I get it.

I have watched you for thirty-four years as you transformed in your body and stayed the same. *Exactly*. I have watched you turn and pivot through the many red dances we've been drawn into, toe to toe, our feet like hands.

The rain is falling against the skylight in the living room of this apartment on Bilkova this evening. Though the rain is thick with grey, the sky is also bright. There's a sun close by. The pigeons coo and crackle across the red clay tiles. A siren rises and subsides a mile away, beyond the Jewish Quarter.

You are asleep down the hall, your body a complex Russian doll of encasements of interlocking times and versions of you — not as chronological time, but as different bodies of you that lean into different grasses for embraces. You lie there so slight, but contain all those fronds of you that are also there, sleeping, and dreaming.

In one of those dreams a child, a young girl, is painting on watercolor paper in a white room. The child is methodically dipping a brush in then out of an old pickle jar full of discolored water, careful to squeeze out just the right amount of water from the brush hairs each time on the lip of the glass. And then the child dips the moist brush into the bright-red tablet in her metal painting case and begins to move the brush on the rough-surfaced bone-white and slightly damp paper. A bird whistles somewhere through an open window. The heavy smell of spring lilacs invades the room. The girl is smiling. She is dreaming herself a princess in an old European city, asleep in a tower, awaiting the prince. He is climbing a dark, circular staircase to reach her. He is always climbing those stairs.

Yesterday we toured the Jewish Museum and Synagogue and, most marvelous, the ancient Jewish cemetery here in Josefov. In the museum we saw a room of children's art that had been rescued from the Terazin Concentration Camp during World War

Two. A small white card beneath each of the paintings indicated whether that child had survived or not.

I watched you pause at each of these paintings. You have taught so many children art over the years I have known you. I watched you disappear into those paintings, those lives. You knew instinctively what was being whispered and celebrated in each case.

Eventually, hand in hand, we descended the stone spiral stairs of the synagogue and out of the gallery and down onto the bright streets of Prague. We had coffee in the Franz Kafka Café. We walked the cobblestone streets as young lovers might, transformed by love, by being *in the world*.

I am sitting just down the hall from you right now, writing. You are asleep, dreaming. I am always climbing stairs to reach you. Those children. Dark spiral staircases, everywhere. Lilacs. I am the heavy, rough paper. Your eyes see something unfolding on me: you are smiling at a bright-red narrative. The dewlap brush hairs caress my stretching skin and it all begins to happen again. Of *course*. I get it.

*Acknowledgements*

I would like to thank Thistledown Press for first publishing "Outside the Sylvia" in 1990 in *The Face in the Garden*; *Canadian Poetries* and Shawna Lemay for publishing "Atomistic Plates" in 2013, *The Ryga Journal* and Sean Johnston for publishing "Four Cubist Sonnets" in 2011; *Literature/Politics Magazine* and Theresa Smalec for publishing "Hat Trick" in 2018.

I always have a long list of people to thank when a book comes out, and that is simply because there are people in my life who support me in constant and subtle ways and they're important to me. First, I have two wonderful families — my own and Jude's — that make my writing possible. Second, I have a community of writers and musicians who are always a part of my life, too: Natalie Appleton, Vindu Balani, Giles Blunt, Hannah Calder, Corinna Chong, Michelle Doege, Jason & Curtis Emde, Neil Fraser, Kerry Gilbert, Betty Johnson, Sean Johnston, Jake Kennedy, Phil Lambert, Steven Lattey, Fionncara MacEoin, Craig McLuckie, John Murphy, Mark Nishihara, Jay Ruzesky, Greg Simison, Andrew Smith, Glen Sorestad, Sharon Thesen, Shelby Wall, Calvin White, Tom Wayman, and Ron Woznow.

A special thanks to Mary Ellen Holland because she is so often the first reader of my material and buoys me up with her insights and understanding.

Another special thanks to my sister Susan and my brother Harry who lived all those St. Agnes years so closely with me and whose lives are intertwined with mine always. When we first sang together as a group in the mid-60s, I loved knowing that people couldn't tell our voices apart. I sometimes feel the same thing about our lives, these interchangeable mysteries.

*I need to take this opportunity to thank Thistledown Press for allowing me to experience a life in art in such an independent but supported way. From the early 80s, when the wonderful Glen Sorestad and the inimitable Paddy O'Rourke first spotted me, then nurtured me as a writer, to all my subsequent collaborations with Al Forrie and Jackie Forrie, I couldn't have dreamed of a better publisher than Thistledown Press, nor better friends to work with. I know Thistledown is a Canadian publisher whose contribution to Canadian Literature will become clearer and clearer as time goes by, but right now I need to say this press' role in my own life has been immeasurable.*

What a strange and wondrous joy it was for me to have Jay Ruzesky edit this volume of poetry. He was so gutsy and generous and arduous, and completed something in my writing life that was perfect for me in terms of generations and legacy.

And for Jake Kennedy's ear and eye.

And for Jude Clarke, everything.